How
Sele   rs

We dedicate this book to Nima Mohva-Bhatti and Ella Schlesinger

How to Pass
Selection Tests

Essential preparation for numerical, verbal, clerical and IT tests

4th edition

Mike Bryon & Sanjay Modha

KoganPage

LONDON PHILADELPHIA NEW DELHI

First published in 1991
Revised edition 1992
Title changed to *How to Pass Selection Tests* in 1994
Second edition 1998
Third edition 2005
Fourth edition 2010
This edition 2011

120 Pentonville Road	1518 Walnut Street, Suite 1100	4737/23 Ansari Road
London N1 9JN	Philadelphia PA 19102	Daryaganj
United Kingdom	USA	New Delhi 110002
www.koganpage.com		India

© Mike Bryon and Sanjay Modha 1991, 1998, 2005, 2010, 2011

The right of Mike Bryon and Sanjay Modha to be identified as the authors of this work has been asserted by them in accordance with the Copyright, Designs and Patents Act 1988.

ISBN   978 0 7494 6211 6
E-ISBN   978 0 7494 6212 3

British Library Cataloguing-in-Publication Data

A CIP record for this book is available from the British Library.

Library of Congress Cataloging-in-Publication Data

Bryon, Mike.
  How to pass selection tests : essential preparation for numerical, verbal, clerical and IT tests / Mike Bryon, Sanjay Modha.
    p. cm.
  Rev. ed. of: How to pass selection tests : essential preparation for numerical, verbal, clerical and IT tests. 4th ed. 2010.
    ISBN 978-0-7494-6211-6 – ISBN 978-0-7494-6212-3 1. Employment tests. I. Modha, Sanjay. II. Title.
    HF5549.5.E5B78 2011
    650.076–dc22

                                                                    2010041927

Typeset by Graphicraft Ltd, Hong Kong
Printed and bound in India by Replika Press Pvt Ltd

Contents

Introduction

In recent years there has been a huge increase in the use of selection tests. The increase has been particularly pronounced in the area of employment with many more employers now relying on a test to help them decide between candidates.

As well as becoming far more popular, the style and method of testing has also changed. In a test today the questions are more likely to describe work situations, and their relevance to the job will be much more obvious. Far more common are questions about your personality and preferred working style. A test these days may well be taken at a computer terminal although tests administrated with paper and pen are still very common.

Tests have changed over recent years but you still need to be well prepared to succeed. Lots of practice is essential if you are to show your full potential in a selection or psychometric tests and this is why this book is so valuable. It contains many hundreds of really relevant questions that will allow you to prepare for the most common tests in use today. If you are applying for work in an office environment, in business, finance, administration or media then you will find it essential preparation.

The Kogan Page testing series includes titles aimed at all levels and most areas of testing. This book is the ideal starting point for a candidate facing tests at the intermediate level. Recommended sources of further practice are also provided.

The idea for this book arose from our work in pre-employment training for some of the largest employers in the UK. Our work involved preparing people for the selection process of these organisations and the posts that they would go on to fill. This experience led us to conclude that many people who fail the tests could in fact pass them. What is required is that they come to terms with their anxieties and prepare well prior to the test.

The purpose of this book is to make available to a general readership the strategies developed while preparing candidates for the selection tests.

Since its publication in 1991, *How to Pass Selection Tests* has become a best-seller and proved of considerable help to thousands of people who face employers' tests. This fourth edition ensures that the exercises continue to help candidates prepare for the challenge of selection tests.

Motivated candidates complain that they are unable to obtain sufficient practice material. In response to this we have added over 200 new practice questions and added explanations to some of the answers. You will find material relevant to the majority of tests in use today and by working through the book you will revise essential skills and competencies.

Together with the editors we have tried to ensure that there are no errors in this book. If you find one then please accept our apologies and be kind enough to inform us of it so that it can be removed from the next imprint.

If you are finding it difficult to locate practice questions relevant to the test you face then feel free to contact us through Kogan Page and if we know of a source then we will be happy to provide you with details.

CHAPTER 1

Aims of the book

Many companies and organisations use tests for selection purposes and for many people these tests represent a significant obstacle to obtaining the job or career of their choice. The aim of this book is to inform readers about these tests and provide exercises so that they can practise before sitting a test. Over half the book comprises exercises that are relevant to some of the most common types of selection test currently in use.

Practice can result in significant improvements in performance in most sorts of test. It also boosts confidence and helps individuals to cope with nervousness. It makes individuals less prone to mistakes and ensures that the test is approached proficiently.

Information is provided about the history and nature of tests, and explanations are offered about why companies use tests and what they believe can be concluded from the results. Advice is also given about what to do if you fail.

CHAPTER 2

General information about tests

History of tests

The first standardised test of ability was produced in France at the beginning of the last century by Binet. Initially, the tests were developed for use with children for diagnostic purposes. It was not until World War I that testing for adults really began. These tests proved to be valuable in selecting and allocating recruits for different types of work in the armed forces and also for identifying potential officers. During World War II further advances in selection methods were made. Once again, the tests proved to be valuable in allocating different people to a variety of jobs or trades at different levels or grades.

There were certain advantages in using paper and pencil tests in groups (these are also applicable today in industry and commerce). First, it allowed a large number of people to be tested in one sitting. Second, it allowed people to be tested under the same types of conditions, ie, the physical conditions and instructions could be standardised. Third, people could be allocated to jobs or trades for which they had the aptitude rather than simply being rejected or allocated to jobs on the basis of a simple interview – which can be very subjective.

The use of tests in the two wars played an important part in classifying large numbers of people. Since then tests have been developed and adapted for the needs of industry and commerce. Many organisations, particularly the larger ones, now regularly use selection tests because of the advantages referred to above and other advantages to which we shall refer in a later section (see page 11).

What are selection tests?

Selection tests, as the name suggests, are tests that are designed and used for the purpose of selecting and allocating people. The tests can be used in a number of situations; for example, in selecting people for jobs, in promoting or transferring people to other departments or jobs, and in certain types of course. They are also used in redundancy and career counselling and are known as psychometric or psychological tests.

Psychometric tests are one way of establishing or confirming an applicant's competence for the job. They can be useful provided they are reliable and valid for the job for which they are being used. Selection tests are standardised sets of questions or problems that allow an applicant's performance to be compared with that of other people of a similar background. For example, if you happen to be a graduate your score would be compared to those of other graduates, or if you have few or no qualifications your score would be compared to people who are similar to you, and so on. What this means is that the tests are norm referenced (the section dealing with results explains what this means – see page 13).

Reliability and validity

We said that tests can be useful if they are reliable and valid. So what do these two words mean in this context? It is said that a test is *reliable* when consistent results are obtainable. For example, tests that contain ambiguous questions are likely to be unreliable because different people will interpret the questions differently, or even the same person may interpret them differently on different occasions.

Tests are said to be *valid* when they measure what you want them to measure. In personnel selection terms it means that a test must be related in some way to the known demands of the job if it is to be of any use. For example, it needs to be shown that a test score predicts success or failure in a given job.

Figure 2.1 illustrates the kind of relationship that ought to exist between test scores and job performance in which the higher the test score the better the performance in the job. In reality, however, it would be almost impossible to find such a high positive correlation. This is because of the difficulties in measuring job performance in many, if not most, types of job.

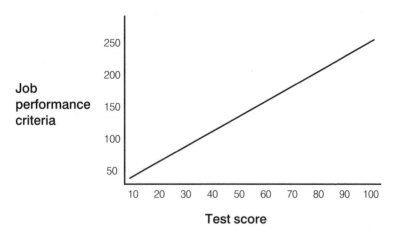

Figure 2.1   A positive correlation between test scores and job performance

Different types of test

In this section we shall look at the various types of psychometric tests and questionnaires that are used. These are attainment and aptitude tests (work sample and trainability tests are also aptitude tests) and personality and interest inventories.

Ability tests

Ability is the most common aspect of a candidate that is subject to testing, either in the form of paper and pencil tests or some practical exercise. These practical tests are sometimes referred to as performance tests or work sample tests; another variation of these are the trainability tests. We shall deal with these later (see page 8).

Ability tests fall into two main categories: attainment tests and aptitude tests. Aptitude is having either a talent for a particular skill or the potential to acquire it. Attainment is the candidate's current skills and knowledge. It needs to be pointed out that the distinction between attainment tests and aptitude tests is not clear-cut. This is because a single test can be used to measure either attainment or aptitude.

Attainment tests

Attainment tests are those that seek to assess how much skill and knowledge an individual has. For example, an arithmetic test for supermarket cashiers measures attainment as long as it is used to measure arithmetic and not to measure performance as a cashier.

From an employer's point of view an attainment test may provide a better assessment than simply looking at a past record of achievements or non-achievements as the case may be. A standardised test of arithmetic or spelling may give a more reliable indication of relevant present ability than a comparison of school qualifications in maths or English.

From a candidate's point of view an attainment test score will say more to an employer than simply talking about his or her skills. This is particularly useful when the candidate does not possess many, or even any, qualifications.

Aptitude tests

Aptitude tests are used to predict the potential of an individual for a particular job or a course of study. However, as mentioned above, it is not easy to separate tests of potential from tests of attainment because all forms of test assess the person's current skills and knowledge. But the results of that assessment may then be used in a variety of ways. For example:

- to highlight the individual's strengths and weaknesses;
- to provide career counselling;
- to predict success in a job or course.

Work sample tests

Work sample tests are no different from the paper and pencil aptitude tests except that they are practical. They are a miniature version of the job in question. The tasks encompass the main or major elements of a job. They are called work sample tests because that is the main purpose, hence they are sometimes referred to as performance tests.

Trainability tests

Another variation of the work sample test is the trainability test. Trainability testing is a method of assessing applicants' potential for learning new skills in a particular area by carrying out a practical exercise.

Personality questionnaires (tests)

Many people refer to personality inventories or questionnaires as tests. This, however, is misleading because to talk about personality questionnaires as tests implies that there is a pass or fail score, which is not the case.

Personality is something that everyone talks about. You often hear people talking about someone having a 'great personality', but what exactly is it?

There is no one theory or definition of personality with which all psychologists agree, but most personality questionnaires aim to identify certain stable characteristics. They are based on the assumption that the responses to be given will be a representative sample of how an individual will respond in a given social situation, particularly the one in which the selector is interested, ie, the organisation or department in which that individual may be working.

The main characteristics that personality questionnaires aim to identify in an individual are:

Extroversion	Introversion
Tough minded	Tender minded
Independent	Dependent
High self-confidence	Low self-confidence

Interest inventories (tests)

Strictly speaking, interest tests like personality tests are not tests at all, because they are not about obtaining a good or a bad score, or about passing or failing. It is for this reason that they are usually referred to as interest inventories or interest questionnaires. The aim of these interest inventories is to find out an individual's interest in particular occupations.

Interest inventories cover interests in activities such as:

Scientific/technical	– how and why things work or happen
Social/welfare	– helping or caring for people
Persuasion	– influencing people and/or ideas or selling goods and services
Arts	– designing or creating things or ideas
Clerical/computing	– handling data, systems

The use of interest inventories is limited compared to, say, aptitude tests in the selection of applicants. This is because the inventories appear, at least on the face of it, easy to fake. For example, if a person is applying for a position as a clerk, he or she may deliberately indicate a stronger interest in tasks related to the office environment. The interest inventories are probably most useful in vocational guidance where one assumes that people are less likely to fake them.

Fair and unfair discrimination

All good tests discriminate! That, after all, is the purpose of the test. However, this discrimination should be on the basis of ability, and is therefore fair and legal discrimination. If the tests, or the way in which they are used, discriminate on the basis of sex or race it would be unfair and possibly even illegal under the Sex Discrimination and the Race Relations Acts.

It does not matter whether the unfair discrimination is intentional or unintentional. However, the Acts do not explicitly refer to testing. The implication of the two Acts is that if the use of the tests (or other selection methods) results in proportionately more women or members of the ethnic minority communities 'failing' the test and as a result not being taken on and the use of the test cannot be justified, this may be unfair discrimination. The onus of proof is on the employer to justify the use of the test.

For example, if an employer sets a condition (let us say a test score of X or above) and a larger proportion of women or ethnic minority groups fail to meet this condition, compared with men or the ethnic majority group, the employer may be required to show that this condition is necessary. If the use of the test can be shown to be justified, the result would be fair discrimination.

When an employer uses tests to select employees, it is on the understanding that the test will differentiate between those candidates with and those without the appropriate skills, knowledge and potential. A test that does not differentiate between the level of abilities in candidates is of no real value to the employer. It is important to the employer that the right person is chosen for the right job. It is equally important to the candidate that it is the right job for him or her. Otherwise the candidate may not be happy in the job or, even worse, he or she may not be capable of doing the job, which can be very demoralising. Fair discrimination is about distinguishing between people, based on their abilities and aptitudes. These must be shown to be related to the job for which the tests are being used. What this means in practice is that if an employer uses a particular test to identify a given set of abilities and aptitudes, these must be shown to be necessary to do the job. For example, it may need to be shown that high scorers do well in the job in question and that low scorers do not.

We mentioned the Sex Discrimination Act and the Race Relations Act. These two Acts, which have much in common, have identified two types of discrimination: direct and indirect. Direct discrimination is where an employer treats someone unfavourably or indeed favourably because of his or her sex, colour or ethnic background. Such discrimination is unlawful. Indirect discrimination is where an employer sets a condition that a large proportion of a particular group fail to meet, eg, women or people from ethnic minority groups. This type of discrimination could be held to be unlawful if the condition set by the employer is not necessary or justified.

Why companies use tests

There are a number of advantages to companies and other organisations in using psychometric tests. These include:

1 Where an organisation receives a large number of applications, and because most selection tests are paper and pencil types, applicants can be tested in large groups. This, of course, is much more cost-effective.

2 The recruitment and selection process can be a costly affair, particularly if there is a high turnover of staff because of bad

selection decisions, not to mention any other disruptions that may be caused. Thus it is in the interests of the company to choose the right people for the job. The use of tests can help in this process, provided that the tests are both valid and reliable.

3 Tests can also lessen subjectiveness in assessing the applicant's potential to develop his or her aptitude for a particular job. The lessening of subjectiveness in the selection process is also an advantage for applicants.

4 The use of tests with other selection procedures can lead to better and fairer decisions on the part of the employer.

Test conditions

Most tests are conducted under strict 'examination'-type conditions. The main reason for this is to ensure that all candidates, at all times, are tested in the same manner. This is so that no group being tested is either advantaged or disadvantaged in terms of receiving the test instructions.

The process followed will be laid down by the test publishers. However, the majority of tests are likely to be conducted in the following way:

1 All candidates will be sitting facing the test administrator.

2 Candidates will be provided with all the materials necessary, such as pencils, eraser, answer sheets, rough paper (if allowed by the test publisher).

3 The tester will explain the purpose of the test(s) and also inform candidates how the test will be conducted.

4 The tester will read the instructions to be followed for the test. These instructions may also be written on the test booklet, in which case they should be read at the same time. In some tests the candidates are left to read the instructions by themselves.

The reading time may be included in the test time or extra time may be given.

5 For the majority of tests, if not all, there is a strict time limit that the tester will adhere to. The tester may use a stopwatch; don't be put off by this. Interest inventories and personality questionnaires do not usually have a strict time limit, though candidates are asked to complete them as quickly as possible.

6 Many tests have example questions. In some tests the candidates are asked to attempt these, while others have them already completed. In any case, their purpose is to ensure that the candidates understand what is required of them.

7 In most tests, candidates are given the opportunity to ask questions. If you do not understand what is required of you, you should seek clarification. You should not feel intimidated about asking questions, no matter how trivial the question may seem to you. The chances are that there are other people who have similar questions but who haven't plucked up enough courage to ask them. So the motto is – ask; you have nothing to lose!

How the results are interpreted

So far we have talked about different types of test. Now we need to address the issue of what happens once you have taken the test.

Naturally, they are scored; that is, they are marked. Once scored, the correct answers are added together. The result is called a raw score. If there is more than one test all the raw scores are noted. A set of tests is called a battery of tests.

The raw score does not really mean anything on its own. This is because it does not tell us whether it is a good or a bad score. Let us assume that candidate A gets 30 questions right out of a possible 50. So candidate A has a raw score of 30. If the test is easy and most people who are similar to him or her would have scored around 40, A's score is bad. On the other hand, if the test is a difficult one and most of the other people would only have scored around 20, candidate A's score is a good one.

Thus, in order for the scores to be meaningful, we have to compare the individual's score with that of a similar group of people. We would then be able to say that, compared to those people, this individual is either average, above average or below average. We make this comparison by using what are called norm tables. Norm tables tell us how other people have scored on a test. The group with whom we would compare an individual's score is called a norm group and test norms are the norm group's scores. In a norm referenced test the raw scores are compared with a norm group.

CHAPTER 3

What to do if invited to sit a test

Why practice helps

If you and some friends were invited to enter a competition to change the wheel of a car in the shortest possible time and your team had practised, you would expect to be faster as a result. Your team would be less prone to mistakes and you would set about the task in a far more effective way.

Practice can lead to improvements in performance in most sorts of test, including those used by companies during selection. By how much your score might improve depends on a number of things. One is the amount of practice that you undertake; another is the quality of the material on which you practise (it must be similar to the real test). An important variable is whether you have had much previous experience of selection tests. The candidate who is new to tests stands to show the most improvement, while someone who has had lots of test experience may show little or no improvement.

The most important single factor that will decide by how much you improve your score through practice is you! To improve, you have to be motivated. From our experience, doing well in a selection test is not simply a matter of intelligence or aptitude: you also have to try hard and you must have a certain amount of self-confidence.

As we have said, not everyone will show an improvement; if you have taken lots of selection tests you may show little or none. Equally, anyone who is a poor reader or weak at maths may need to attend literacy or numeracy classes before any noticeable improvement. But for many, practice will make a significant contribution and in some cases will allow you to pass what you would otherwise have failed.

Whether practice will make the difference in a particular instance depends on where you are starting from. If you would have passed anyway, practice may only help you to obtain a slightly higher score. If you would have failed with a very low score, you may not be able to improve enough to pass, no matter how much you practise. However, you may be among the large number of candidates who fail a selection test by only a few marks and 12 to 16 hours' practice may mean that, instead of failing, you pass.

The way to look at it is this. What have you got to lose? Spending, say, two hours a night for six nights practising for a test can only help and it might make all the difference.

There is evidence to suggest that practice does help. For example, a woman who had twice failed the Civil Service test for Administrative Assistants, and had been trying to get an administrative job in the Civil Service for over a year, enrolled on a course that provided a total of five days' test practice. At the end of the course she sat the test and passed.

Make a decision

You have to decide how much you want the job. If you decide that it is something you really want you should make up your mind to attend the test! It is not unusual for as many as 40 per cent of the candidates to fail to show up on the day. You are also going to have to set aside some time to prepare for the test.

If, in your search for work, you have experienced a lot of rejection it is going to take courage to make the level of commitment that we ask.

Establish a clear idea of the test demands

The company or organisation that invites you to take a test will most likely include with the invitation a test description. This is an important source of information. If you do not receive such a description, telephone the company and ask if you can be sent details.

It is essential that you establish from the test description a clear idea of what the test involves and select exercises with similar demands. To help ensure that you do indeed have a clear idea, try the following exercise.

Familiarise yourself with the test description to the point at which you are able to describe in your own words each section of the test. For example, you ought to be able to state how many sections the test consists of, how long you are allowed for each section and what you have to do in each. If you are unable to do this you are not sufficiently familiar with the test description, so continue to read it to yourself until you can describe each section in your own words.

Ask someone else to read the description sent by the organisation and explain to him or her your account of what you are going to have to do. If your friend accepts your account of the test, you've got it.

Seek out relevant material

If the test involves maths and English exercises the majority of the material in this book will be of use. However, if the test is designed to measure, for example, coordination, dexterity, perceptual skills or abstract mental reasoning, you will need to obtain additional material. Likely sources are books with exercises purporting to measure IQ (intelligence quotient) or offering an assessment of aptitude. Libraries and career services may be able to lend you copies. If the test measures specialist knowledge seek out textbooks on the subject, especially those that end sections with questions and answers. Libraries of colleges of further education may be a good place to begin your search. If you are not a student you will probably not be allowed to borrow books, but no one should mind you using the library for reference purposes. You will find a list of further relevant titles on the Kogan Page website (www.koganpage.com).

Prepare a programme of work

Once you have a clear idea of the test demands and sufficient practice material you need to plan when and where you are to practise.

You should practise for no more than two hours at a time and allow some time fairly close to the test. The benefits of practice are short-lived so practise right up to the day before the test. Although some is better than none, you should aim to undertake a minimum of 12 hours, and perhaps as much as 20 hours, of practice. The factor that will probably decide how much practice you do will be the amount of relevant material that you can obtain.

Always work somewhere quiet and don't listen to music or watch television at the same time. Your programme of work ought to look something like this:

- You are notified that you are going to have to sit a test.

- You undertake a study of the test description (two hours).

- You search for relevant practice material.

- You undertake a series of two-hour practice sessions (10 to 18 hours).

- You take the test.

Coach yourself

Work through the material that you have obtained at your own pace without consulting the answers. Then go over it with the answers, trying to work out why the answer is the one given, rather than simply seeing how many you have got right; that way you are learning. Put the material aside and move on to other material; after a few days go through the original material again, this time against the clock (you might give yourself a minute an exercise). By following this method you will go over the material three times under a combination of conditions.

The night before the test

Lack of sleep or illness will affect your score detrimentally. You need to get a good night's sleep before the test. If you are unwell telephone the organisation to see if you can sit the test at a later date. Do not drink alcohol before a test.

Test anxiety

Do you get worried before taking a test? Do you tend to think you are not doing well while taking a test?

Test anxiety is quite a common problem for most people. The only difference is the degree to which people worry. Generally, it has been found that a slight amount of anxiety is a good thing; however a large amount can be detrimental.

Too much worry and too many negative thoughts can draw attention away from the task in hand – that of taking the test – and thereby disrupt performance. On the other hand, a little anxiety is beneficial: it will help you to be more alert and help your performance.

If you are one of those people who worry too much and have negative thoughts about your performance during a test, you will need to learn how to relax. You will also need to be more positive.

After all, failing a test is not the end of the world – though it may seem like it at the time!

Test strategies

How you conduct yourself during the test is of utmost importance. There are a few golden rules.

Probably every test paper in the country advises the candidate against spending too long on a particular question. It is good advice. If you do not think you are going to be able to answer a question, move on to the next and if there is time come back to the questions that you have missed.

It is important that you place your answer in the correct place on the answer sheet or test booklet. If the test has an answer sheet separate from the questions, take particular care to check regularly that the question number corresponds to the number against your answer.

It is equally important that you indicate your chosen answer in the way requested. If the instructions ask you to, for example, tick the correct answer, make sure you do tick your choice rather than perhaps circle it or underline it.

Guessing sometimes pays. If the test is a multiple-choice paper and you do not know the answer, it may pay to guess. If, for example, you have to choose from four possible answers guessing would allow you to get, on average, one question in four right. Often you can improve on this average because you are sometimes able to recognise one or more of the suggested answers as incorrect.

Estimating sometimes helps in multiple-choice maths tests. Rather than working out inconvenient sums it is quicker if you round the amount up or down to a convenient number.

What to do if you fail

We have coached a lot of people through a range of selection tests and know for certain that failure does not necessarily mean that you are unable or do not have the ability to do the job. All it definitely means is that you failed the test! You may be perfectly able to do the job and pass the test if you took it a second or third time. The thing to do is not to give up.

Most companies will not tell you your score or allow you to retake the test straight away. In some cases you are not allowed to retake the test for six months and you will have to reapply, which involves filling out the application form, and so on, all over again. This means that you have time to improve your English or maths so that you pass the test the next time.

It will help if, straight after the test, you sit down and try to remember as many of the questions as you can. Then go and find some exercises that remind you of the test. We suggested earlier the kinds of place you might find them.

Now test yourself on the examples that you managed to find; try to be honest and, if you do really badly, it may be that the only way you are going to improve is to attend classes at a college of further education. If you attended for a year you might obtain sufficient qualifications to exempt you from having to do the test again!

Some of the most common types of test

In this chapter, descriptions are given of some of the most common kinds of test and their demands are illustrated with examples. Further practice material is provided in Chapter 5.

You are most likely to encounter the following types of test:

● *Verbal reasoning*. These are about how well you understand ideas expressed in words and how you think and reason with words.

● *Numerical reasoning*. Like the verbal tests these aim to identify strengths in understanding, only in this case it is your strength in understanding and reasoning with numbers.

● *Diagrammatic reasoning*. These deal with diagrams.

● *Mechanical reasoning*. These deal with mechanical concepts.

● *Abstract reasoning*. These seek to identify how good you are at thinking in abstract terms, ie, dealing with problems that are not presented in a verbal or numerical format.

- *Clerical skills*. These deal with checking and classifying data, speedily and accurately.

- *Personality questionnaires*. These involve a series of statements about, for example, your working style, attitude towards risk and approach to planning. You have to indicate if you agree or disagree with them.

- *Situational tests*. These are very similar to personality questionnaires but you are provided with a description of an imaginary situation and a series of statements relating to it. You must indicate if you agree or disagree with the statements if you found yourself in that situation.

All the practice material provided in this book relates to the verbal, numerical and clerical types of test. If you are interested in diagrammatic tests of reasoning, you will find practice material in the following three books useful: *How to Pass Computer Selection Tests, How to Pass Diagrammatic Reasoning Tests* and *How to Pass Technical Selection Tests* (all published by Kogan Page).

Nearly all these tests will have a time limit. But we have not imposed time constraints in this chapter because it is more important that you become familiar with the tests, and this is best done under relaxed conditions where you work at your own pace. Later you will find exercises that allow you to practise against time.

Verbal tests

Tests that measure comprehension

These tests set out to establish if the candidate can demonstrate a level of understanding of written language. They can involve, for example, swapping or finding missing words, choosing between sentences, or identifying words that have the same or opposite meaning.

Tests that assess spelling

Most spelling tests require you to indicate which words in a list are incorrectly spelt. In some cases you are provided with a list of correctly spelt words from which you are able to check the spelling. You may have either to write or underline the correct spelling or look the word up on a correctly spelt list and write down the corresponding number.

Tests of grammar and punctuation

Grammar demonstrates the relations between words, while punctuation serves to divide and emphasise. It is quite common for tests of grammar and punctuation to examine also your command of spelling and comprehension.

Tests of logical thinking

These tests are intended to measure the candidate's ability to follow instructions or work out relationships between numbers, shapes, figures or statements and predict, for example, what comes next.

Numerical tests

The purpose of these tests is to examine your grasp of the four fundamental operations of arithmetic: addition, subtraction, multiplication and division. We later refer to these as the four rules. Sometimes the test also investigates the candidate's handling of percentages and fractions. You are not usually allowed to use a calculator, slide rule or any other sort of aid. These tests may also require the candidates to apply their grasp of arithmetic to a series of practical situations or demonstrate their understanding by estimating the answers.

Tests of clerical and computing skills

There are many tests that try to predict whether a candidate is suited to work with computers or as a clerk. For example, the tests investigate the candidate's ability to check information, follow coded instructions or rules, sequence events into a logical order and interpret flow diagrams.

Practice examples

The following pages provide practice examples of some of the most common types of test. Do not worry if you cannot do some of the examples. If you get stuck ask someone to help. Answers are given on pages 000–000.

1. Verbal tests that measure comprehension

A. Swapping words

Comprehension tests sometimes consist of single sentences or pairs of sentences that either do not read sensibly or have a word or words missing. You have to make the sentences sensible by swapping words or you have to complete a sentence by choosing words from a list.

Examples of swapping words:

Tick the two words that if swapped would make the following sensible.

> you have to try test to do well in a hard.

Note that in this type of test you must only switch two words and from wherever you move the first word the other must go. Sometimes the question consists of two sentences, one of which requires no revision.

Now try this example:

Tick the two words that if swapped would make the following sensible.

> limit all tests impose a time virtually

B. Finding missing words

If the sentence has a word or words missing you are expected to indicate which word or words are needed to complete the sentence, usually from a number of suggestions.

Examples of missing words:

> The .....sat on the.....

A mat, cat   B cat, mat   C mat, mat

Answer [   ]

C. Locating words that mean the same or the opposite

Comprehension-type selection tests sometimes test a candidate's grasp of synonyms (words in the same language that mean the same) or antonyms (words that mean the opposite of each other or are contradictory). For example:

> famous means the same as:

A tropical   B distress
C celebrated   D skater

Answer [   ]

> kind means the opposite of:

A generous   B callous   C ideal
D heavy   E frantic

Answer [   ]

2. Tests of grammar and punctuation

These tests often involve the candidate having to choose which of a number of sentences are correct or, alternatively, choose from a number of words, or pairs of words, which will correctly complete a sentence.

A. Choosing from a number of sentences

In each of the following two examples, choose which sentence is correct and place its letter label in the answer box.

A Where would you go to buy shoes.

B Where would you go to buy shoe?

C Where would you go to buy shoes?

D Where would you go to buy shoe's?

Answer

A A yacht is a type of boat that has sails.

B A yacht is a type of boat which that sails.

C A yacht is a type of boat who has sails.

D A yacht is a type of boat who that sails.

Answer

B. Choosing from pairs of words

Choose which pair of words correctly fits the spaces in the incomplete sentence.

Thomas and.....visit you yesterday.

A me will   B I will

C me did   D I did

Answer

Try this example:

.....were.....policemen to every protester.

A Their, too   B There, to

C Their, two   D There, two

Answer

3. Spelling tests

These tests require you to identify which words are either correctly or incorrectly spelt. Sometimes you have to write out the correct spelling or underline either those correctly or incorrectly spelt. It is important that you pay attention to the instructions otherwise you may make the error of, for example, underlining the correct spellings when you were asked to underline the incorrect ones. Try the following examples:

Example 1. Underline the *correct* spellings.

Wedesday	Febuary	indecate	butiful
sincerely	foreign	sataday	archetec
immediate	equiped	merchandise	juvenille
deliverys	mashinery	shampoo	responcibility

Example 2. Where the spelling is wrong write the correct spelling in the space alongside.

author	....	balence	....
beeutify	....	corelate	....
desease	....	foremost	....
holiday	....	occasion	....

Example 3. Below is a list of 25 words, spelt correctly and in alphabetical order. There then follow two groups of seven words. In each of these groups there may be up to three spelling errors. Your task is to find the word or words that are incorrectly spelt. Once you have found these words, locate them in the first list in which spellings are correct and write their numbers in the answer box. Your answers do not have to be in numerical order. One of the answers has been given.

List

1. among	11. hasten	21. warranty
2. balance	12. hypocrisy	22. writing
3. calendar	13. imprecise	23. yield
4. creative	14. knuckle	24. yourself
5. delayed	15. league	25. zeal
6. disturb	16. numerous	
7. emphasis	17. plasticity	
8. equality	18. receive	
9. forgery	19. secretary	
10. generous	20. vacuum	

1

calendar	hypocrisy
recieve	balance
amoung	vacum
yourself	

Answer [1 | |]

2

zeal	warrantie
delaiyded	generous
plasticity	hasten
secretery	

Answer [| |]

4. Tests of logical thinking

Sometimes you have to follow instructions in this type of test or you may be expected to work out relationships and then make a prediction.

A. Following instructions

There are a wide number of variations on this type of test. The instructions you have to follow often include the alphabet and numbers. These types of question may or may not be multiple-choice. Here is a useful tip: with this sort of question it helps if you take one clause at a time. Try these examples:

Example 1

> If Wednesday comes before Friday and May comes before December, place the second letter of the alphabet in the answer box. Otherwise place the first letter of the word Wednesday in the answer box.

Answer

Example 2

> Divide the largest figure by the smallest and then add the result to the second figure from the left. Enter the letter that matches your result in the answer box.

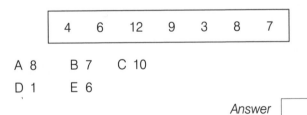

| 4 | 6 | 12 | 9 | 3 | 8 | 7 |

A 8   B 7   C 10
D 1   E 6

Answer

B. Relationships between numbers and statements

In this sort of question you have to say what you think logically fits the gap or will come next. Sometimes you are expected to identify which is the odd one out from a collection of numbers, words or shapes. Try these examples:

Example 1. What number fits the gap?

> 7   11......19   23

Answer

Example 2. Which is the odd one out?

> A The Isle of Wight
> B Anglesey
> C Skye
> D Stoke on Trent

Answer

Example 3. Which is the odd one out?

> 5   25   16   40

Answer

Example 4. Which is the odd one out?

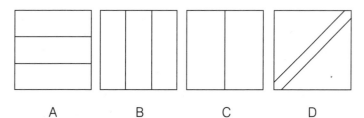

A   B   C   D

Answer

5. Numerical tests

Most numeracy tests require you to complete a variety of sums that will test your command of the four rules: addition, subtraction, multiplication and division. Try the following examples without using a calculator. Do not worry if you get stuck; there are lots more practice examples given later in the book.

A. Numerical reasoning

Some companies are concerned that you can not only carry out basic mathematical calculations but also apply them in practical situations. To test this ability they use the following kinds of question.

Example 1

If a first class stamp costs 30 pence, how much would 50 first class stamps cost?

Answer [ ]

Example 2

If the balance of petty cash is £93.70 before you were instructed to purchase stationery to the value of £20.18 what would be the new balance?

Answer [ ]

Example 3

Fourteen people attended the annual office party and the cost was £350. How much is that per head?

Answer [ ]

Example 4

The office photocopier service contract is charged at 1.4 pence each copy. How much would be charged for 1,500 copies?

Answer [ ]

B. Estimating/approximating

This type of test sets out to measure your ability to approximate the answer to calculations. Usually, this type of test is multiple-choice and the amount of time allowed does not allow you to work out answers exactly. Try these examples:

Example 1

48 + 55 =

      A 1113   B 33   C 203   D 103   E 93

Answer [   ]

Example 2

12 × 9 =

      A 108   B 78   C 128   D 1108

Answer [   ]

C. Percentages and other fractions

In addition to the four rules discussed and illustrated above, some tests also examine your command of fractions and percentages. The questions may take any of the forms so far covered. For example:

Example 1

$$\frac{1}{2} + \frac{2}{3} + \frac{1}{4} =$$

Answer [   ]

Example 2

$$\frac{1}{4} + 2\frac{1}{3} + \frac{1}{2} =$$

      A $3\frac{1}{12}$ B $2\frac{1}{12}$ C $1\frac{1}{12}$ D $\frac{1}{12}$

Answer [   ]

Example 3

> Your employer asked if you would work overtime at time and a
> half. Your normal rate of pay was £4.50 an hour. How much an
> hour would you earn while working overtime?

Answer [   ]

Example 4

> The cost of a new fax machine was £640 without value added
> tax. If the tax was 17.5%, how much would the total cost of the
> fax machine be?

Answer [   ]

Example 5

> What is 24% of £380?

Answer [   ]

Example 6

> Estimate 65% of 350. Enter the letter corresponding to
> your answer in the box.

A 508   B 227.5

C 58   D 1208   *Answer* [   ]

6. Tests of clerical and computing skills

These tests attempt to measure a candidate's aptitude for computing
and clerical work. You may have to sit them as part of a battery of tests
that could include verbal and numerical tests as described above.

They include following coded instructions, interpreting flow diagrams, suggesting the appropriate sequence of events, and checking that data has been accurately inputted. Try the following examples:

A. Flow diagrams

Flow diagrams are used to represent a sequence of events, their interconnections and outcomes. Study the flow diagram below; it represents the opening of a computer file. Use it to answer the question.

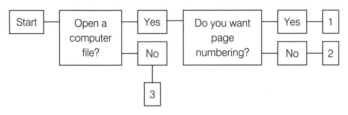

Question

A user wishes to open a file without page numbering. Which outcome does the user require: 1, 2 or 3?

Answer

B. Sequencing

These are tests in which you have to put a set of items or instructions into a defined order. Sometimes the items are everyday things like going to work or they may be particular to computing. Try the following:

Write what you believe is the correct order for these events in the answer box.

Word processing

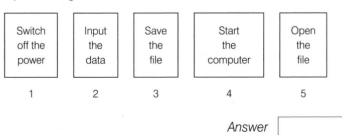

Answer

C. Coded instructions

This type of question involves sets of rules that you have to interpret and then apply. Try the following example:

Below are a set of codes and their meanings. You have to use this information to answer the series of questions.

Code

To open a file	OF
To copy a file	CF
To leave the program	ESC
To delete a file	DF
To check the spelling in a file	SP
To save a file	SF

Questions

What is the code:

1   To open a file?

Answer [   ]

2   To delete a file and leave the program?

Answer [   ]

3   To open a file, check the spelling and save the file?

Answer [   ]

D. Checking computer data

In these tests you are provided with both the original information and a computer printout. You have to check to see whether the data has been accurately inputted on to the computer files.

Example:

In this example you have to check line by line the computer data against the original. If you find any discrepancies mark the answer box with the letter N; if the line has been accurately copied mark the box with the letter Y.

The answer to the first example has been given below.

Original information

1	Land Sales Ltd	9 Lancia Place	Lancaster Gate	ES2 5HJ
2	Fox Associates	143 West Side	Ealing	5HJ 6TT
3	Colliers Building	68 Cambridge Street	Queens Way	3DD 5TG
4	Top Creation	11 George Road	Plaistow	9NN 4RF
5	Victoria Packing Systems	34a Major Street	Great Hardwood	2DE 6VC
6	Municipal Supplies	22 Warehouse Road	Small Heath	8MN 6AS
7	Berton Hotel	78 Baker Street	Uxbridge	12FD 5TT
8	Save Finance	53 Church Yard Close	Sherman	7FC 4DX
9	Longsdale Ltd	2 Burton Street	Hackney	E5 2CD
10	Western Electronics	10 Resister Road	East Ham	E6 4RF
11	New Technologies	13 Fourth Avenue	Manor Park	E12 5NT
12	Net Surfing Cafe	20 Cyber Street	Compton	CB13 7FG
13	Super Robotics Plc	145 Wells Street	High Grove	HG8 2WL
14	Info Tech Ltd	1 New Lane	Hertfordshire	NW3 2SA
15	Printer Printers	2 Print Street	Printington	PT5 2PR

1

Land Scales Ltd	N
9 Lanca Place	N
Lancaster Gate	Y
ES2 5HJ	Y

2

Fox Associates	
143 West Side	
Ealing	
5HJ 6TT	

3

Collers Building	☐
68 Cambridge Street	☐
Queeens Way	☐
3DD 5TG	☐

4

Top Creation	☐
11 Gorge Road	☐
Plaistow	☐
9NN 4RF	☐

5

Victoria Pack Systems	☐
34a Major Street	☐
Great Harwood	☐
2DE 6VC	☐

6

Municipal Supplies	☐
22 Warehouse Road	☐
Small Health	☐
8MN 6AS	☐

7

Barton Hotel	☐
78 Baker Street	☐
Uxbrige	☐
12DD 5TT	☐

8

Save Finances	☐
53 Church Yard Close	☐
Sherman	☐
7FC 4DX	☐

9

Longsdale LTD	☐
2 Burton Street	☐
Hackney	☐
E5 2CD	☐

10

Western Electronic	☐
10 Resister Road	☐
EastHam	☐
E9 4RF	☐

11

New Technology	☐
13 Forth Avenue	☐
Manor Park	☐
E12 5NT	☐

12

Net Surfing Cafe	☐
20 Cyber Street	☐
Compton	☐
CB13 7FG	☐

13

Super Robotics PLc	☐
145 Well Street	☐
High Grove	☐
HG8 2WL	☐

14

Info Tech Ltd	☐
1 New Lane	☐
Hertfordshire	☐
NW3 25A	☐

15

Printers Printers	☐
2 Print Street	☐
Printington	☐
PTS 2PR	☐

When you check your answers, go over the exercises that you got wrong again and see if you can work out your mistake.

7. Personality questionnaires

These involve a long series of statements and you need to say whether you agree or disagree with them. They include lots of statements such as:

I find it easy to start a conversation with a complete stranger.

Strongly agree
Agree
Disagree
Strongly disagree

This style of question is becoming very common, and employers use it to help select people who will fit into the working style of their organisation, or who indicate that they have the qualities needed to succeed in a position. They usually occur early on in an application process, and they are sometimes completed online or feature as part of an application form.

There is not usually a definite right or wrong answer to this style of question, as the answer will often depend on the organisation and position to which you are applying. If you were applying to work in a call centre in which you were required to telephone members of the public (and had never spoken to them before), then the employer would be looking for people who would agree with the example statement above.

Take these questionnaires seriously because many people don't pay sufficient attention to them, and they can be used to reject a large number of applicants. Before you complete a personality questionnaire be sure to first find out about the preferred working style of the company to which you have applied. Decide if it is the kind of place you would like to work then set about answering the questions in such a way that shows you to be the ideal candidate.

Avoid indicating that you agree or disagree strongly with too many questions because if you do you risk suggesting that you hold many strong opinions and the employer might fear that you would find it difficult to join their team.

Answer the questions truthfully but always answer them in the context of how you would act if you were working for the company in the vacant role. Be careful not to answer a question as if were you out with your friends and might not be as professional and courteous as you are at work. For example, you may come across a statement that reads:

> I like to joke around.
>
> Strongly agree
> Agree
> Disagree
> Strongly disagree

Most employers would be put off by a candidate who agreed with this statement. In the workplace they do not want too much joking around. So, if you are the life of the party and a fantastic practical joker when out with you friends be sure to answer the questionnaire within the context of how you act when at work, where most practical jokes are considered inappropriate.

8. Situational tests

These tests are similar to the personality questionnaire but they provide you with a series of practical situations, and your task is to say how you would respond if you found yourself in that situation. In some instances there is a passage of information describing the context of the questions that follow. For example:

> **Context**
> You have been working very hard to complete an assignment and have been coming into work early all week and have taken shorter lunch breaks than usual in order to get the job done. No one else in the team has done this and at last the job is done. Your manager does not seem to have noticed the commitment you have shown and you can't help but feel a little disappointed in the lack of recognition. You add up all the extra time you have worked this week and realise it amounts to an extra day's work.

Situational questions

1   You would take Monday off and phone in pretending that you feel too unwell to come into work.

    Strongly agree
    Agree
    Disagree
    Strongly disagree

2   The next time there is an assignment to complete you would not come in early and would take your full lunch break.

    Strongly agree
    Agree
    Disagree
    Strongly disagree

3   You would approach you manager and discuss how you feel with him.

    Strongly agree
    Agree
    Disagree
    Strongly disagree

If you have a grievance in work the best thing to do is to raise it with your manager at the first sensible opportunity. For this reason most employers would prefer that you answer the three questions above by disagreeing with the first two but agreeing with the third.

Once again be careful not to make the mistake of forgetting that these questions are about how you might act at work and not how you might act if you were out and about at the weekend. Take the example:

> If I found £20 I would not hesitate to pick it up, keep it for
> myself and think myself very lucky.
>
> Strongly agree
> Agree
> Disagree
> Strongly disagree

Many people will agree with the above statement as it would probably be almost impossible to find the person who has lost the
money. However, at work where there is every possibility that the
person who lost the money could be found, most employers would
prefer that their staff respond to the situation by handing the money
in so that it might be claimed by the unlucky person who mislaid it.
For this reason most employers would expect you to disagree with
this statement.

You will find a 100 question practice personality questionnaire and
further advice in *Ultimate Psychometric Tests* (published by Kogan
Page).

CHAPTER 5

Practice material

This chapter consists of practice exercises relevant to some of the most common types of test currently used for selection purposes. The exercises are divided into three categories: verbal, numerical and clerical.

Time limits have been suggested for some of the exercises and answers can be found on pages 000–00. When you check your answers try not to see simply how many questions you got right; instead, go back over the questions and try to work out why you went wrong. That way you are learning.

Verbal tests

1. The same meaning or the opposite

Underline the word that has the same meaning and circle the word that has the opposite meaning as the first word on the *left*. For example:

elastic   (brittle)   hidden   <u>stretchy</u>   action

Try these:

store	stockpile	sieve	tent	waste
wrong	nail	catch	mistaken	right
question	answer	misery	describe	enquire
measure	artery	volume	guesswork	gauge
problem	absent	concave	solution	obstacle
obscure	objective	transparent	conceal	colourful
synthetic	man-made	music	thought	natural
vertical	horizontal	upright	topmost	summit
repair	impair	neglect	recondition	test
strengthen	lengthen	purify	augment	weaken

If you do not know the answers to any of these examples look them up in a dictionary. You could also try a Thesaurus, which lists synonyms (words that mean the same). Once you have finished the exercise, why not make up some examples of your own?

Your grasp of synonyms and opposites may be tested in a variety of ways. Here are some examples of the way these types of question are worded. Try them and make up examples of your own.

You have to underline the correct answer.

1   Car is to motor boat as bike is to:

> pedalo   rowing boat   sailing boat   submarine

Now make up an example of this type of question yourself:

.... is to .... as .... is to: ....

2   Skill means the same as:

> weak   ability   inept   cunning

Make up an example of this type of question:

.... means the same as:

....

3   Which of the following means fight?

> brute   burn   brawn   brawl

Make an example:

Which of the following means ....?

....

4   Hard is to soft as stone is to:

> rock   water   mud   marble

Make up an example of this kind of question:

.... is to .... as .... is to: ....

5   Long means the opposite of:

> high   low   short   wide

Make up an example yourself:

.... means the opposite of:

....

2. Sound alike/look alike words

Some words have different meanings but sound identical or very similar, for example:

site (place) and sight (view)

Other words again have different meanings but look similar, for example:

dairy (milking shed) and diary (memoir)

Words that sound or look like other words are often used in verbal selection tests and it is surprising how often the same examples come up. It may help if you are clear over the difference between the meaning of some common examples.

Use a dictionary if necessary to be clear about the difference in meaning between the pairs of words below. Then make up sentences that demonstrate the difference. For example, in the case of site and sight:

Sentence 1.   The site is over on the left.

Sentence 2.   It rained all the way and by the time they arrived they were quite a sight.

Now write a sentence for the word 'cite', which also sounds like site and sight.

Sentence 3.   ....

....

Be sure you understand the difference in meaning of these sound alike/look alike words.

Exercise 1

morning mourning	ascent assent	principal principle
be bee	here hear	edition addition
whether weather	right write	piece peace
course cause	except accept	brake break
specific Pacific	meet meat	advise advice
boar bore	allowed aloud	excess access
effect affect	council counsel	though through threw
practice practise	waist waste	for fore four
stationary stationery	there their	

You have **two** minutes in which to place the correct pairs of words from the above lists into the gaps in the sentences below.

1   We .... down on him.

       The .... was in the cage next to the elephant.

2   You need to be more .... in the use of your words.

       We looked out across the .... Ocean.

3   He went this ....

       She is in ....

4   It was the .... of the matter.

       We had to do it, after all she was the ....

5   I was up to my .... in it.

       It seemed so wrong that there was so much ....

6   .... I waited for over half an hour.

       The sound of some words gives an indication of .... meaning.

Exercise 2

You are presented with a number of sentences. In each sentence you will find two or more words placed in brackets. Your task is to choose one word that best completes the sentence and write it in the space provided.

1   All the guests (knew, new) each other at the party.

       ....

2   There was (to, too, two) much traffic on the motorway.

       ....

3   In a South American country the (guerrillas, gorillas) were on the verge of gaining control of the capital city.

       ....

4   The (rap, wrap) on the door caused John to awaken from his dream.

....

5   There were only a (few, phew) television sets left in the shop.

....

6   Louise was asked to collect the (draft, draught) from the bank on her way to work.

....

7   It was all (quiet, quite) on the Western Front.

....

8   All the (writes, rights, rites) were performed by the local priest.

....

9   That building was built in the 17th century and was originally an (arms, alms) house.

....

10   In the old days, water pipes were made from (led, lead).

....

11   The gale force wind was (effecting, affecting) the television reception.

....

12   They found it difficult to decide (whether, weather) to go to Spain or to France for the holiday.

....

13   The lorry driver (accepted, excepted) that it was his fault.

....

14   It was a great (feet, feat) that the climbers achieved.

....

15   She placed the bottles over (there, their, they're) on the table.

....

16   To quote is to (cite, site, sight).

....

17   The computer should not be switched (of, off) until the disk has been removed.

....

18   The surgery was full of (patients, patience) waiting to see the doctor.

....

19   The postman put the letters (through, threw) the letterbox.

....

20   At the interview Jane was asked to take a (sit, seat).

....

21   Children should be seen and not (heard, herd).

....

22   Kathy said her voice felt very (horse, hoarse).

....

23   The postman always brings the (male, mail) at 8.30.

....

24   The (scene, seen) from the hilltop was magnificent.

....

25   Everyone went to the party (accept, except) James.

....

26   When the phone rang, Jane and Chris were on (there, their, they're) way out to the shops.

....

3. Choosing the right word

In many verbal tests you have to choose a word from a number of options that you believe completes the sentence correctly. Try the following examples:

Instructions

You have to choose a word from the box that in your opinion correctly completes the sentence, then write that word in the space.

1 I left the car over ....

> there, their

2 I could not have .... another thing.

> eaten, ate

3 .... the post arrived yet?

> has, have

4 It looks .... it is going to rain.

> like, as, as though

5 .... was it her fault.

> or, nor

6 I knew .... it was going to happen.

> that, what

7 We .... talking when he interrupted.

> were, was

8   My sister and .... went to see our grandmother.

me, I

4. Timed exercise – choosing the right word

Over the page you will find 10 questions. Before you turn over, set a clock or watch to allow yourself **five** minutes to complete them.

Instructions

Choose from the suggested answers the words that you believe correctly complete the sentence and write them in the space provided.

It could be a question of either spelling, grammar or meaning.

Do not turn the page to begin the timed exercise until you are ready.

1   They all .... that she was ....

> knew, leave, new, gnu, leaving, leafing

2   .... should .... seen them.

> ewe, you, had, have

3   She is a very .... young ....

> abel, able, women, woman

4   I do hope the .... will be ....

> weather, whether, fine, fined

5   We .... this morning.

> flew, flu, flue, accross, across

6   We must .... to ....

> agreement, agree, agreed, differ, difer

7   My eyes are .... from looking at the ....
screen.

> tied, tyred, tired, colour, colore

8   The results are given in the .... and ....
below.

> colum, column, rows, roes, rouse

9 Can this .... be .... on our computer?

> program, programme, uses, used

10 The .... called and asked if you would phone back.

> centre, centaur, manger, manager

END OF EXERCISE

5. Choosing the right sentence

Sometimes verbal tests require you to choose a sentence rather than a particular word. This type of test can examine your command of punctuation as well as grammar, spelling and syntax (meaning). Try the following examples:

1 A. I thought that their was a problem with the laser printer?

B. I thought that there was a problem with the laser printer.

C. I through that their was a problem with the laser printer.

D. I through that they're was a problem with the laser printer.

Answer [   ]

2 A. The matter will be given immediate attention.

B. The matter will be given mediate attention.

C. The matter will be given mediate attension.

Answer [   ]

3 A. In response to the interest you have expressed in our product
         I enclose the relevant information, order form and price list.

     B. In responce to the interest you have expressed in our product
         I enclose, the relevant information, order form and price list.

     C. In responce to the interest you have expressed in our product
         I enclose the relevant information order form and pice list.

                                        Answer [   ]

4 A. The most common form of dismissal involves the termination
         of a worker's contract with notice.

     B. The most common form of dismissal involves the termination
         of a workers' contract with notice.

     C. The most common form of dismissal involves the termination
         of a workers contract with notice.

                                        Answer [   ]

5 A   Childcare facilties have being made available.

     B. Childcare facility have been made available.

     C. Childcare facilities have been made available.

     D. Childcare facilities has been made available.

                                        Answer [   ]

Here is a useful tip: it helps if you not only look for the correct answer
but also try to rule out some of the sentences by recognising them
as incorrect.

Over the page are 10 further examples of this type of question. Check
your watch and allow yourself **five** minutes to complete them.

Do not turn the page to begin the timed exercise until you are ready.

6. Timed exercise – choosing the right sentence

1 A. There is the man whom represents the company.

B. There is the man which represents the company.

C. There is the man who represents the company.

D. There is the man what represents the company.

Answer [＿＿＿＿＿＿]

2 A. Luckily the error was discovered before the end of the physical year.

B. Luckily the error was discovered before the end of the fiscal year.

C. Luckily the era was discovered before the end of the fiscal year.

D. Luckily the era was discovered before the end of the physical.

Answer [＿＿＿＿＿＿]

3 A. In the enclosed envelop you will find the reciept.

B. In the enclosed envelope you will find the receipt.

C. In the enclosed envelope you will find the reciept.

D. In the enclosed envelop you will find the receipt.

Answer [＿＿＿＿＿＿]

4 A. David said John is late.

B. 'David said' John is late.

C. David said, 'John is late.'

D. David, 'said John', is late.

Answer [＿＿＿＿＿＿]

5   A. The committee sat much later than expected.

      B. The comittee sat much latter than expected.

      C. The committee sat much later than accept.

      D. The committe sat much later than expected.

Answer [ ]

6   A. I like Fridays and I hate Mondays.

      B. I like Fridays both I hate Mondays.

      C. I like Fridays nor I hate Mondays.

      D. I like Fridays but I hate Mondays.

Answer [ ]

7   A. There really is an access of filing to be done.

      B. There really is an excess of fileing to be done.

      C. There really is an access of fileing to be done.

      D. There really is an excess of filing to be done.

Answer [ ]

8   A. Try not to allow your expenditure to exceed what you urn.

      B. Try not to allow your expenditure to accede what you earn.

      C. Try not to allow your expenditure to exceed what you earn.

      D. Try not to allow your expenditure to excess what you earn.

Answer [ ]

9   A. Colin was born on the 19th August, at King Street Hospital Manchester, his father was at work.

      B. Colin was born on the 19th August, at king street hospital Manchester his father was at work.

      C. Colin was Born on the 19th August at King Street Hospital manchester his Father was at Work.

      D. Colin was born on the 19th August at King Street hospital Manchester his father was at work.

E. Colin was born on the 19th August, at King Street Hospital, Manchester; his father was at work.

Answer [   ]

10 A. The delivery of stationary is two days late.

B. The delivery of stationery is too days late.

C. The delivery of stationary is to days late.

D. The delivery of stationery is two days late.

Answer [   ]

END OF EXERCISE

You might find it useful to go back over these exercises at your own pace.

7. Plural words

You are given a word for which you have to find the correct plural spelling from a list on the right-hand side. Now try this and see how you get on.

1 Interview   A. Interviewees
                    B. Interviewers
                    C. Interviews
                    D. Interviewes
                    E. None of these

Answer [   ]

2 Vacancy   A. Vacancys
                  B. Vacancyes
                  C. Vacancise
                  D. Vacancies
                  E. None of these

Answer [   ]

3   Shelf   A.   Shelfs
                    B.   Shelves
                    C.   Shelfes
                    D.   Shelvses
                    E.   None of these

Answer [   ]

4   Match   A.   Matchees
                    B.   Matches
                    C.   Matcheses
                    D.   Matchses
                    E.   None of these

Answer [   ]

5   Business   A.   Business
                    B.   Businesses
                    C.   Businessis
                    D.   Businessies
                    E.   None of these

Answer [   ]

6   Monkey   A.   Monkees
                    B.   Monkeyes
                    C.   Monkeies
                    D.   Monkies
                    E.   None of these

Answer [   ]

7   Family   A.   Familys
                    B.   Familyes
                    C.   Familese
                    D.   Families
                    E.   None of these

Answer [   ]

8 Message A. Messages
B. Messagess
C. Messagies
D. Messagees
E. None of these

Answer

9 Donkey A. Donkeyes
B. Donkeyies
C. Donkeies
D. Donkies
E. None of these

Answer

10 Photocopy A. Photocopis
B. Photocopyes
C. Photocopyis
D. Photocopies
E. None of these

Answer

11 Ability A. Abilitys
B. Abilityes
C. Abilites
D. Abilities
E. None of these

Answer

12 Capacity A. Capacites
B. Capacitis
C. Capaciteis
D. Capacities
E. None of these

Answer

13 Adjective   A. Adjectives
                   B. Adjectivies
                   C. Adjectivees
                   D. Adjectivyes
                   E. None of these

Answer [   ]

14 Allegory   A. Allegores
                  B. Allegories
                  C. Allegoryes
                  D. Allegoryies
                  E. None of these

Answer [   ]

15 Ambiguity   A. Ambiguities
                   B. Ambiguityes
                   C. Ambiguitys
                   D. Ambiguites
                   E. None of these

Answer [   ]

16 Antique   A. Antiquies
                 B. Antiques
                 C. Antiqueys
                 D. Antiqueis
                 E. None of these

Answer [   ]

17 Customer   A. Customeres
                  B. Customerse
                  C. Customers
                  D. Customeries
                  E. None of these

Answer [   ]

18 Disguise   A. Disguises
          B. Disguisees
          C. Disguisess
          D. Disguisies
          E. None of these

Answer [ ]

19 Euphemism A. Euphemismes
          B. Euphemisms
          C. Euphemismse
          D. Euphemismies
          E. None of these

Answer [ ]

20 Hoof   A. Hoofs
          B. Hoovs
          C. Hoofes
          D. Hooves
          E. None of these

Answer [ ]

21 Guarantee A. Guaranteies
          B. Guaranteses
          C. Guarantees
          D. Guaranteis
          E. None of these

Answer [ ]

22 Machine   A. Machinies
          B. Machines
          C. Machinees
          D. Machins
          E. None of these

Answer [ ]

23   Negative   A.   Negatives
                            B.   Negativeis
                            C.   Negativies
                            D.   Negativees
                            E.   None of these

Answer ☐

24   Personality   A.   Personalities
                            B.   Personalites
                            C.   Personalitees
                            D.   Personalityes
                            E.   None of these

Answer ☐

25   Platitude   A.   Platituds
                            B.   Platitudes
                            C.   Platitudus
                            D.   Platitudas
                            E.   None of these

Answer ☐

26   Psychologist   A.   Psychologistes
                            B.   Psychologists
                            C.   Psychologisties
                            D.   Psychologistees
                            E.   None of these

Answer ☐

27   Rhyme   A.   Rhymies
                            B.   Rhymes
                            C.   Rhymses
                            D.   Rhymeies
                            E.   None of these

Answer ☐

28 Sequence A. Sequences
               B. Sequencees
               C. Sequenceies
               D. Sequencies
               E. None of these

                                        Answer [_____]

29 Taxi   A. Taxies
               B. Taxis
               C. Taxise
               D. Taxes
               E. None of these

                                        Answer [_____]

30 Roof   A. Roofs
               B. Roovs
               C. Roofes
               D. Rooves
               E. None of these

                                        Answer [_____]

31 Sense   A. Senseces
               B. Sencees
               C. Sensies
               D. Sensees
               E. None of these

                                        Answer [_____]

32 Thief   A. Thiefes
               B. Thieves
               C. Thievse
               D. Thiefves
               E. None of these

                                        Answer [_____]

33 Statesman A. Statesmans
B. Statesmens
C. Statesmen
D. Statesman
E. None of these

Answer

34 Technology A. Technologyes
B. Technologies
C. Technologys
D. Technologees
E. None of these

Answer

35 Language A. Languagies
B. Languagees
C. Languagese
D. Language's
E. None of these

Answer

8. Spelling

Below is a list of 75 words, spelt correctly and in alphabetical order.

On the following pages you will find groups of nine words. In each group there may be up to four spelling errors. Your task is to find the word or words that are incorrectly spelt. Once you have found these words, locate them in the first list in which spellings are correct and write their numbers in the answer box. Your answers do not have to be in numerical order.

For your assistance an example has been given. Study the example and then complete the eight questions.

1 Abbreviate	**26** Earring	**51** Illustrate
2 Absolute	**27** Economically	**52** Impatient
3 Accountant	**28** Egalitarian	**53** Inadmissible
4 Alternative	**29** Eligible	**54** Incompatible
5 Autumn	**30** Emperor	**55** Inflammable
6 Beautiful	**31** Equilibrium	**56** Jostle
7 Beneficial	**32** Exaggerate	**57** Junction
8 Billiards	**33** Failure	**58** Ladder
9 Boutique	**34** February	**59** Language
10 Broadcast	**35** Fiction	**60** Laughter
11 Brutus	**36** Flotation	**61** Leadership
12 Bustle	**37** Formula	**62** Magistrate
13 Canada	**38** Functionalism	**63** Manage
14 Carburettor	**39** Gallon	**64** Marginal
15 Category	**40** Geometric	**65** Mercury
16 Caterpillar	**41** Gesture	**66** Middle
17 Centrifugal	**42** Goggle	**67** Minimum
18 Complementary	**43** Gradual	**68** Monetary
19 Defeatism	**44** Graphology	**69** Napkin
20 Definite	**45** Handkerchief	**70** Neighbour
21 Designer	**46** Harbour	**71** Nightingale
22 Develop	**47** Hexagon	**72** Northern
23 Devotee	**48** Homogenous	**73** Nucleus
24 Diffidence	**49** Hospital	**74** Numerous
25 Diplomatically	**50** Humiliate	**75** Nurture

For example:

Brodcast	Fiction	Leadership
Handkerchief	Formular	Earing
Hospital	Napkin	Hexagon

10	37
26	

In this example there are only three errors, but as explained there can be up to four.

1   Minnimum   Gradual   Centriugal
       Deffinite   Northern   Jostle
       Exaggerate   Defeatism   Homegenous

       □ □
       □ □

2   Absolute   Ecconomically Benefitial
       Brutus   Napkin   Fiction
       Ladder   Goggle   Mercury

       □ □
       □ □

3   Language   Boutique   Failure
       Gallon   Gestture   Devotee
       Impatient   Febuary   Nurture

       □ □
       □ □

4   Busle   Caterpillar   Complementary
       Desiner   Humiliate   Marginal
       Harbor   Manage   Canada

       □ □
       □ □

5   Laughter   Graphology   Flotation
     Geometric   Catagory   Deffinite
     Hospital   Nightingale   Middle

☐ ☐
☐ ☐

6   Egaletarian   Josle   Develop
     Homogenous   Nucleaus   Accountant
     Canada   Illustrate   Inflamable

☐ ☐
☐ ☐

7   Autum   Harbour   Neighbour
     Defaetism   Emparor   Ladder
     Billiards   Gallon   Numerious

☐ ☐
☐ ☐

8   Failure   Minnimum   Nightingale
     Devalop   Humiliate   Northern
     Mercurey   Carburettor   Difidence

☐ ☐
☐ ☐

9. Timed spelling

Over the page are 10 further examples of this type of question. Check your watch and allow yourself **10** minutes to complete them.

Do not turn the page to begin the timed exercise until you are ready.

1 Alternate	**26** Knife	**51** Quintillion
2 Amalgamation	**27** Kitchen	**52** Radiate
3 Anaesthesia	**28** Lagging	**53** Rampage
4 Analogous	**29** Latitude	**54** Rapture
5 Appeasement	**30** League	**55** Recital
6 Arbitrary	**31** Magazine	**56** Rendezvous
7 Assessor	**32** Mansion	**57** Ridiculous
8 Broach	**33** Minister	**58** Safeguard
9 Bullion	**34** Nitrate	**59** Satellite
10 Ceremonious	**35** Nominate	**60** Scaffolding
11 Chancellor	**36** Numeration	**61** Scientist
12 Dismantle	**37** Nutritious	**62** Scratch
13 Diversity	**38** Oath	**63** Segregate
14 Exhaustion	**39** Obsession	**64** Solemnize
15 Expedient	**40** Omission	**65** Tangible
16 Flippant	**41** Orchestra	**66** Technician
17 Frustrate	**42** Pantomime	**67** Temporarily
18 Genealogy	**43** Parochial	**68** Tongue
19 Guillotine	**44** Penicillin	**69** Undulate
20 Hereditable	**45** Petition	**70** Utility
21 Humility	**46** Pneumonia	**71** Variety
22 Indentation	**47** Pygmy	**72** Velvet
23 Invention	**48** Quadrangle	**73** Warranty
24 Journal	**49** Quicken	**74** Wealthiness
25 Justify	**50** Quinine	**75** Xylophone

1   Alternate   Broch   Petition
        Neumonia   Pigme   Tongue
        Rampage   League   Minister

☐ ☐
☐ ☐

2   Flippant   Justify   Outh
        Valwet   Asessor   Quicken
        Safegard   Rapture   Invention

☐ ☐
☐ ☐

3   Exhustion   Kitchen   Manshun
        Nitrate   Recital   Justify
        Bullion   Chansellor   Varity

☐ ☐
☐ ☐

4   Amalgamation   Technician   Obsession
        Geneology   Journul   Knife
        Magazine   Humility   Radiate

☐ ☐
☐ ☐

5   Zylophone   Penicillin   Orcastra
     Pantomime   Parocail   Utility
     Ceremonious   Anaesthesia   Omission

☐ ☐
☐ ☐

6   Warranty   League   Appesement
     Divercity   Guillotine   Scientist
     Tanjible   Temporarily   Latitute

☐ ☐
☐ ☐

7   Hereditable   Indentation   Resital
     Frustrate   Dismantel   Arbitary
     Omission   Rondevous   Nominate

☐ ☐
☐ ☐

8   Ridiculuous   Scraach   Expedient
     Segregate   Numeration   Petition
     Quinine   Satallite   League

☐ ☐
☐ ☐

9 Quadangle   Solemize   Lagging
     Rapture   Obsesion   Nitrate
     Alternate   Undulate   Warrantee

10 Nutritious   Rapchure   Welthiness
     Hereditable   Indentation   Latitude
     Scaffolding   Flippant   Temprarily

END OF EXERCISE

10. Reading for information

You are presented with some passages to read. A number of statements follow each passage. Your task is to say whether the statement is true or false. The statement can only be true if the information in the passage bears this out.

Example:

The great fire of London started in Pudding Lane, near London Bridge, in the year 1666. It was probably the worst fire in the City's history.

1 The great fire of London took place in 1666.

    <u>True</u> or False (underline one of these)

When the American War of Independence started, the Americans had no regular army. But one was soon formed under the command of George Washington. However, this army was badly equipped and lacked proper training.

The war lasted for six years, from 1775 to 1781, and the Americans drew up the formal Declaration of Independence on 4 July 1776. This stated that the United States would be an independent republic.

1   The highly trained American army quickly won the war.

True or False

2   The war lasted for six years and the Declaration of Independence was made shortly after the end of the war.

True or False

3   The first regular American army was commanded by Washington.

True or False

The brain begins to show signs of decline after a certain proportion of the nerve cells of which it is formed have died. As people get older they have fewer and fewer nerve cells, because once the cells have died they are not replaced.

By the time a person reaches the age of 75 as many as a quarter of the nerve cells may have died.

Although science has advanced a great deal and scientists today are better placed to study how our brain functions, there is still a great deal to discover.

4   By the time a person is in his mid-seventies he may have lost as many as 25 per cent of his nerve cells.

True or False

5   Scientists today are able to cure the dying nerve cells, because of the great advances made by science.

True or False

6 The brain cells, like the skin cells, are able to multiply and that is why all the brain cells do not die out.

True or False

The problem with the notion of technology is that there are various meanings of the term. It no longer has a precise and limited meaning, but rather a vague and expansive one.

The term is used to describe not only instruments and machines but also skills, methods and procedures, among other things.

Some commentators have argued that technology is a factor that determines key facets of organisations.

However, others have argued that there is no cause and effect relationship between adoption of the technologies and the structural and performance outcomes that may be associated with them.

7 Everyone agrees with the single definition of technology.
True or False

8 When people talk about technology they are always referring to machines, such as computers.
True or False

9 Some people have argued that technology is a determining factor in a number of key areas of an organisation.
True or False

For more (and more difficult) examples of this type of question, see *How to Pass Graduate Psychometric Tests* (published by Kogan Page).

A different style of reading for information question

In the following questions you are given a series of passages each of which is followed by a number of statements. It is your task to say whether the statement is true or false or whether it is not possible to say if the statement is true or false. You should base your decision only on the information or opinions given in the passage.

You should judge the statement to be true only if, for example, it follows logically from the passage or is a rewording of something contained in the statement or is a valid summary of the statement or a part of it.

You should judge the statement to be false if it, for example, cannot follow logically from the statement or if it contradicts something contained in the passage.

If you require further information than is contained in the passage before you can tell if the statement is true or false then you should record your answer as cannot tell.

Passage 1
Our solar system has nine planets, each of which orbits the sun in an anticlockwise direction on the same plane so forming a disc-shaped system. The four inner ones, Mercury, Venus, Earth and Mars, are spheres of rock while the four much larger outer planets, Jupiter, Saturn, Uranus and Neptune, are gigantic balls of gas with liquid and solid cores. Pluto is the exception in that it is the most distant of the planets from the sun but is, like the inner planets, made up of a sphere of rock rather than a large amount of gas, as are its distant neighbours. All the outer planets and two of the inner planets have at least one moon. Saturn has the most with 20.

1   Mercury is the planet closest to the sun.
True
False
Cannot tell

Answer [   ]

2   Pluto has at least one moon.
True
False
Cannot tell

Answer [   ]

3   There are four outer planets.
True
False
Cannot tell

Answer [   ]

4   Mars is further from the sun than Jupiter.
True
False
Cannot tell

Answer [   ]

Passage 2
High blood pressure or hypertension is caused by poor diet, drinking too much alcohol and obesity. It can be reduced by losing weight, improving one's diet, taking exercise and drinking moderate amounts of alcohol. Hypertension is believed to be the single most common contributor to early death in adults worldwide as it causes heart and kidney disease. It is estimated that 1 billion people suffer from high blood pressure and that the number of sufferers is forecast to increase further still both in developed and developing countries.

5   The incidence of high blood pressure is on the rise around the world.
True
False
Cannot tell

Answer [   ]

6   One billion people will die worldwide from high blood pressure.
True
False
Cannot tell

Answer   [   ]

7   Hypertension is irreversible.
True
False
Cannot tell

Answer   [   ]

8   The rise in cases of high blood pressure will be more marked in developed countries.
True
False
Cannot tell

Answer   [   ]

Passage 3
In some parts of the world the interval between high water or high tide is one day while in other parts of the world there are two high tides every 24 hours. The difference in height between high and low water varies greatly depending on the location. In some places the range can be almost 10 metres, while other places experience a range between high and low water of only approximately a metre or less. These tides are caused by gravitational and centrifugal force. Despite the sun's immense mass it is the much closer moon that provides twice the sun's gravitational pull on the world's oceans. This lunar force causes the water to be drawn to the side of the Earth facing the moon. On the opposite side to the moon a second bulge of water occurs caused by the centrifugal force created by the spin of both the Earth and the moon. It is these bulges of water that are the high tides.

9   The gravitation pull of the sun does not affect the world's oceans.
True
False
Cannot tell

Answer _____

10   The location where the interval between high and low water is one day also experiences the greatest range between high and low water.
True
False
Cannot tell

Answer _____

11   The gravitational pull of moons of Saturn also affects the world's oceans.
True
False
Cannot tell

Answer _____

12   The passage states that centrifugal force causes the ocean to bulge.
True
False
Cannot tell   *Answer* _____

Passage 4

The medieval period lasted from 1000 to 1500. It was preceded by the Dark Ages. Many towns were formed across Europe during this period as trade and populations increased. Kings ruled and with the leaders of the church they decided state affairs. Most people lived in the countryside and worked on the land. They gave a share of their produce to the local lord in return for protection and as rent. They had to work very hard and for much of their lives lived in abject poverty. Life expectancy for the commoner was much shorter than it is today. As a result of the expansion of trade coins became commonplace.

13   The medieval period lasted for 500 years.
   True
   False
   Cannot tell

   Answer   [   ]

14   The majority of the population lived in the countryside.
   True
   False
   Cannot tell

   Answer   [   ]

15   When a harvest failed or was poor the commoner risked starvation.
   True
   False
   Cannot tell

   Answer   [   ]

16   The Dark Ages followed the medieval period.
   True
   False
   Cannot tell

   Answer   [   ]

Passage 5
Radio waves are a type of energy and create electromagnetic fields. They form part of the electromagnetic spectrum, which includes visible light, microwaves and x-rays. We are exposed to many electromagnetic forces, for example when we turn on a light or television. These forces have a heating effect, which is used in a microwave oven to heat food. Mobile phones work by transmitting and receiving

radio waves and because the phone is held close to our heads it is suggested that the heating effect might cause harm to our brains.

17 The passage states that emissions from mobile phones could warm brain tissue.
True
False
Cannot tell

Answer

18 Mobile phones create electromagnetic fields.
True
False
Cannot tell

Answer

19 Radio waves are a part of the electromagnetic spectrum.
True
False
Cannot tell

Answer

20 Children are especially vulnerable because they have thinner skulls and a developing nervous system.
True
False
Cannot tell

Answer

Passage 6
A study in the 1960s followed up in their adult life 800 children who had achieved in psychometric tests of ability scores in the top 1 per cent for their age group. It was reported that 90 per cent of this population had entered university and that 70 per cent had graduated. The study found that the group of adults between them had written 70 books and almost 1,000 scientific papers. Some, however, had served prison

sentences, while others reported unhappy careers and marriages. A second study followed up on very low scoring children. It was found that most when retested as adults obtained scores that were average. A far lower percentage of the low scoring children had gone to university and more reported unhappy careers. The rate for criminal conviction and the incidence of adult mental health problems were reported to be broadly similar across the two groups.

21   Long-term forecasts made from childhood scores in psychometric tests are not very accurate.
True
False
Cannot tell

Answer

22   The passage states that the grades realised at university correlated well with the childhood test scores.
True
False
Cannot tell

Answer

23   The passage suggests that many of the low scoring children as adults had greatly improved their performance in the tests.
True
False
Cannot tell

Answer

24   Most of the differences between these groups in terms of performance in the test and success in work as adults can be attributed to the amount and quality of education received.
True
False
Cannot tell

Answer

Passage 7

The world's population is determined by the balance between the birth rate and the death rate. The population of a particular area can also increase or decrease due to migration. It will increase when the number of immigrants exceeds the number of emigrants and decrease when the number of emigrants exceeds the number of immigrants. The make-up of a population by its age and sex and its life-expectancy will also have implications for the population size and its expected future growth or decline.

25 The world's population overall will not be affected by immigration or emigration.
True
False
Cannot tell

Answer [   ]

26 A higher birth rate will mean a growing world population.
True
False
Cannot tell

Answer [   ]

27 The world's population will continue to grow.
True
False
Cannot tell

Answer [   ]

28 The population of a particular area will decrease if the number of immigrants is higher than the number of emigrants.
True
False
Cannot tell

Answer [   ]

Passage 8

The United States of America is the fourth largest country in the world, the third most populated and the wealthiest. It is made up of 50 states, 48 of which occupy the central part of the North American continent. Its population of 281 million is multiracial as a result of waves of immigrants arriving from Europe, Africa, Asia and South America. Its wealth is derived from its industrial output, its world-leading technologies and science, its extensive agriculture and forestry and vast natural resources including oil, coal and metal ores. It is estimated that something like 45 million tourists visit the United States each year, which makes tourism another very important contributor to the US economy.

29   The passage states that the main languages spoken in the United States are English and Spanish.
True
False
Cannot tell

Answer

30   Its vast industrial output has made the United States the wealthiest nation on earth.
True
False
Cannot tell

Answer

31   The currency used in the United States is the US dollar.
True
False
Cannot tell

Answer

32 The world's fourth most populous nation has a population of less than 281 million.
True
False
Cannot tell

Answer

Passage 9
The Azores are just one of several island groups that are spread across the Atlantic Ocean. To the south lie Madeira and the Canary Islands, the Cape Verde Islands and further south still the Ascension Island and St Helena. Madeira and the Canary Islands are developed holiday destinations visited by tens of thousands of visitors each year. The Cape Verde Islands and the islands further south are much quieter with no sprawling holiday resorts, only traditional villages, giving the visitor the chance to explore remote island life. All the islands share a volcanic geology and have spectacular volcanic coastlines and interiors. Unique and sometimes rare flora and fauna are found on them all.

33 The Azores group are found to the north of the Canaries.
True
False
Cannot tell

Answer

34 The Azores are a developed holiday destination like Madeira with sprawling holiday resorts.
True
False
Cannot tell

Answer

35 The Cape Verde Islands are south of St Helena.

True

False

Cannot tell

Answer [   ]

36 Remote island life can be experienced on the Ascension island.

True

False

Cannot tell

Answer [   ]

Passage 10

Some years ago the Government tried to put into practice the principle that fines for criminal offences should be linked to the income of the offender. People found guilty of a crime had to indicate to which income bracket they belonged and this was used to decide the level of the fine. After a few months the Government withdrew the initiative because it produced some decisions that struck the general public as very unfair. For example, people on very high earnings were fined many thousands of pounds for minor offences while those with no income were fined only a few pounds for some really quite serious crimes. Commentators concluded that the public prefer a system where a fine acts as a deterrent and for this to happen the person fined should to some extent struggle to pay it but at the same time a fine should be proportionate to the seriousness of the offence.

37 A fine of £200 is proportionate to the offence of dropping litter but would be a greater deterrent to someone with a modest income than someone who is rich.

True

False

Cannot tell

Answer [   ]

38 The public prefer a system where the rich are fined thousands of pounds for minor offences.
True
False
Cannot tell

Answer [   ]

39 Under the old system it was possible that two offenders found guilty of the same offence for which they were equally to blame were fined the same amount.
True
False
Cannot tell

Answer [   ]

40 The public no longer hold that fines should bear some relationship to the income of offenders.
True
False
Cannot tell

Answer [   ]

11. Alphabetical order

The alphabet: A B C D E F G H I J K L M N O P Q R S T U V W X Y Z

Arranging words – Example 1

Place the following words in the answer box in alphabetical order:

Gangster   Kidnap
Puff adder   Sorrow
Acrobat   Orator
Heiress   Reptile

Answer

1.	5.
2.	6.
3.	7.
4.	8.

Arranging words – Example 2

Now arrange the following into alphabetical order:

Faithful	Foliage
Fixer	Farmyard
Florida	Fabric
February	Feather

Answer

1.	5.
2.	6.
3.	7.
4.	8.

Rearranging letters

1 Rearrange the letters in 'charity' into alphabetical order. Place your answer in the answer box.

Answer [   ]

2 Rearrange the letters in 'liquor' into alphabetical order. Place your answer in the answer box.

Answer [   ]

3 Rearrange the letters in 'organic' into alphabetical order. Place your answer in the answer box.

Answer [   ]

4   Rearrange the letters in 'Thames' into alphabetical order. Place your answer in the answer box.

Answer [ ]

5   Take the letters that occur in 'Delphi' but not in 'delta' and write them in alphabetical order in the answer box.

Answer [ ]

6   Take the letters that occur in 'kidney' but not in 'kilograms' and write them in alphabetical order in the answer box.

Answer [ ]

7   Take the letters that occur in 'petrol' but not in 'Peru' and write them in alphabetical order in the answer box.

Answer [ ]

8   Take the letters that occur in 'chamber' but not in 'chaise' and write them in alphabetical order in the answer box.

Answer [ ]

Over the page you will find a timed exercise that requires knowledge of alphabetical order.

Before you turn over, set a clock or watch and allow yourself three minutes.

Timed exercise

Instructions

Alongside each name write the file number under which the name should be placed.

The first two examples have been completed.

File numbers

1.	A–Am	10.	J–K
2.	An–Az	11.	L–M
3.	B–Bs	12.	N–O
4.	Bt–Bz	13.	P–Q
5.	C–Ck	14.	R
6.	Cl–Cz	15.	S
7.	D–E	16.	T
8.	F–G	17.	U–V
9.	H–I	18.	W–X,Y–Z

Name	File Number	Name	File Number
Young	18	Warner	
Bayard	3	Carrington	
Harvey		Christie	
Fisher		Tooling	
Skinner		Arnold	
Bishop		Hood	
Adler		Dell	

12. Comparisons 1

1   Man is to boy as woman is to:

A. Lady   B. Girl   C. Madam   D. Lad

Answer [   ]

2   Food is to eat as water is to:

A. Swallow   B. Bathe   C. Drink   D. Shower

Answer [   ]

3   Man is to house as monkey is to:

A. Tree   B. Jungle   C. Cave   D. Nest

Answer [   ]

4 Car is to bicycle as aeroplane is to:

A. Jet   B. Sky   C. Glider   D. Flying

Answer [   ]

5 Ship is to sea as train is to:

A. Station   B. Platform   C. Rail   D. Journey

Answer [   ]

6 He is to him as she is to:

A. She's   B. Her   C. Their   D. Hers

Answer [   ]

7 Cotton is to thread as copper is to:

A. Mesh   B. Wire   C. Electricity   D. Insulation

Answer [   ]

8 Shoes are to feet as gloves are to:

A. Fingers   B. Hands   C. Toes   D. Arms

Answer [   ]

9 Hat is to head as sweater is to:

A. Chest   B. Torso   C. Arms   D. Back

Answer [   ]

10 Floppy disk is to computer as a suitcase is to:

A. Teacher   B. Traveller   C. Technician   D. Trainee

Answer [   ]

11 Sheep is to flock as lion is to:

A. Herd   B. Pride   C. Troupe   D. Leap

Answer [   ]

12 Calf is to elephant as foal is to:

A. Cow   B. Sheep   C. Horse   D. Tiger

Answer [   ]

13 Church is to Christians as temple is to:

A. Jews   B. Muslims   C. Hindus   D. Catholics

Answer [   ]

14 Paper is to tree as glass is to:

A. Pane   B. Sand   C. Stone   D. Clear

Answer [   ]

15 Triangle is to 180 as square is to:

A. 180   B. 240   C. 320   D. 360

Answer [   ]

13. Comparisons 2

Now try the following and see how many you can do in **two** minutes.

1 Pen is to ink as pencil is to:

A. Quill   B. Lead   C. Eraser   D. Crayon

Answer [   ]

2 Black is to white as light is to:

A. Lamp   B. Bulb   C. Dark   D. Bright

Answer [   ]

3 A is to B as Y is to:

A. Z   B. Y   C. X   D. W

Answer [   ]

4 M is to P as G is to:

A. H   B. L   C. J   D. N

Answer [   ]

5 F is to L as R is to:

A. X   B. Y   C. H   D. G

Answer [   ]

6 Eraser is to pencil as Tipp-Ex is to:

A. Chalk   B. Pen   C. Paintbrush   D. Stencil

Answer [   ]

7 Storybook is to read as exercise book is to:

A. Study   B. Doodle   C. Write   D. Draw

Answer [   ]

8 Billy is to nanny as bull is to:

A. Cow   B. Calf   C. Cub   D. Red

Answer [   ]

9 Rectangle is to cuboid as circle is to:

A. Ball   B. Round   C. Sphere   D. Oblong

Answer [   ]

10 Dentist is to teeth as chiropodist is to:

A. Hands   B. Feet   C. Chairs   D. Bones

Answer [   ]

11 Tailor is to clothes as milliner is to:

A. Flour   B. Hats   C. Dressage D. Wheat

Answer [   ]

12 Monarch is to throne as judge is to:

A. Barrister   B. Bench   C. Jury   D. Justice

Answer [   ]

13 Barber is to hair as manicurist is to:

A. Beard   B. Nails   C. Facial   D. Eyelashes

Answer [   ]

14 Optician is to eyes as osteopath is to:

A. Back   B. Bones   C. Ears   D. Nose

Answer [   ]

15 Car is to garage as patient is to:

A. Illness   B. Medication C. Hospital   D. Doctor

Answer [   ]

14. Odd-one-out

1 A. Computer   B. Printer   C. Mouse
  D. Keyboard   E. Monitor

Answer [   ]

2 A. Hands   B. Feet   C. Fingers
  D. Brain   E. Eyes

Answer [   ]

3 A. See   B. Taste   C. Hear
  D. Nose   E. Feel

Answer [   ]

4 A. Wrist   B. Elbow   C. Finger
  D. Thumb   E. Toe

Answer [   ]

5 A. Dry   B. Arid   C. Parched
      D. Desert   E. Swamp

Answer

6 A. Horse   B. Camel   C. Pig
      D. Oxen   E. Elephant

Answer

7 A. Pen   B. Pencil   C. Quill
      D. Chalk   E. Stencil

Answer

8 A. Lion   B. Tiger   C. Leopard
      D. Baboon   E. Cheetah

Answer

9 A. Lantern   B. Lamp   C. Sun
      D. Candle   E. Torch

Answer

10 A. Lake   B. Pond   C. River
       D. Reservoir E. Pool

Answer

11 A. Telephone B. Television C. Facsimile
       D. Telex   E. E-mail

Answer

12 A. Teacher   B. Trainer   C. Lecturer
       D. Instructor E. Examiner

Answer

15. Opposites

1   Down is the opposite of:

A. Horizontal   B. Up   C. Fallen   D. Crouching

Answer [   ]

2   Inflated is the opposite of:

A. Blown-up   B. Deflated   C. Reflated   D. Conflated

Answer [   ]

3   Append is the opposite of:

A. Add   B. Restore   C. Remove   D. Revert

Answer [   ]

4   Correct is the opposite of:

A. Solution   B. Error   C. Right   D. True

Answer [   ]

5   Enter is the opposite of:

A. Come in   B. Arrive   C. Exit   D. Welcome

Answer [   ]

6   Covert is the opposite of:

A. Closed   B. Open   C. Divert   D. Revert

Answer [   ]

7   Restore is the opposite of:

A. Destroy   B. Repair   C. Reinstate   D. Mend

Answer [   ]

8   Drunk is the opposite of:

A. Tipsy   B. Sober   C. Intoxicated   D. Incapable

Answer [   ]

9 Cool is the opposite of:

    A. Freeze   B. Warm   C. Boil   D. Frozen

                                         Answer [ ]

10 Vertical is the opposite of:

    A. Upright   B. Erect   C. Horizontal   D. Upside-down

                                         Answer [ ]

16. Similar sounding words but different spelling and meanings

In this exercise you have to find a word that sounds the same as the word that you are given but is spelt differently.

Exercise 1

For example:

    full   *fool*

1	Sight	....	**2**	Course ....
3	Draft	....	**4**	Broach ....
5	New	....	**6**	Dam ....
7	Weather	....	**8**	Due ....
9	Mail	....	**10**	Die ....
11	Gale	....	**12**	Sweet ....
13	Write	....	**14**	To ....
15	Read	....	**16**	Tail ....
17	Bye	....	**18**	One ....
19	Wave	....	**20**	For ....
21	Need	....	**22**	Flower ....
23	Breach	....	**24**	Sole ....
25	Seen	....	**26**	Hair ....
27	Sun	....	**28**	Heard ....
29	Seem	....	**30**	Heart ....

Exercise 2

See how many you can do in **five** minutes.

1	Fate	....	**2**	Hear	....
3	Great	....	**4**	Hole	....
5	No	....	**6**	Main	....
7	Bored	....	**8**	Ale	....
9	Bold	....	**10**	Night	....
11	Bare	....	**12**	Knit	....
13	Brake	....	**14**	Miner	....
15	Bread	....	**16**	Naval	....
17	Sent	....	**18**	None	....
19	Meet	....	**20**	Or	....
21	Of	....	**22**	Peace	....
23	Peel	....	**24**	Pair	....
25	Peek	....	**26**	Plate	....
27	Pole	....	**28**	Pull	....
29	Pour	....	**30**	Rain	....
31	Pray	....	**32**	Program	....
33	Pearl	....	**34**	Key	....
35	Rest	....	**36**	Rap	....
37	Reek	....	**38**	Ring	....
39	Rye	....	**40**	Shoe	....

17. Written statements/tests

Sometimes when you attend an interview you are asked to write a short statement, of at least 50 words, explaining why you want the job or what you think are the most important aspects of the work. A time limit is imposed.

You are usually told in advance that you will be asked to undertake such an exercise so you can prepare your statement beforehand.

If you know that you are going to have to write a statement, ask someone to help you prepare it. If you keep the sentences short your statement will be easier to read.

Make sure your statement is positive. Consider incorporating, in your own words, points about the work made in the advertisement or information sent to you by the organisation.

You should memorise your statement the night before. Read it aloud again and again, then write it out repeatedly. Keep learning your statement until you are able to write it without notes or prompting. Learn the spelling of any words of which you are unsure.

Try writing your statement in the time that you are allowed – usually 10 minutes – and make sure that your handwriting is neat and legible.

18. Homophones

These are words that sound the same but are spelt differently and have a different meaning.

In this exercise you are presented with a list of words. You are required to find another word that sounds the same but is spelt differently and has a different meaning.

You should try to do these in less than **three** minutes.

1	Him	....	11	Bow	....
2	Sight	....	12	Rung	....
3	Bold	....	13	Pain	....
4	Seem	....	14	Wait	....
5	Been	....	15	Brake	....
6	Ring	....	16	Great	....
7	Right	....	17	New	....
8	Night	....	18	No	....
9	Fought	....	19	See	....
10	Threw	....	20	Where	....

19. More homophones

In this exercise you are again presented with a list of words. You are required to find another word that sounds the same but is spelt differently and has a different meaning.

1	Here	....	**11**	Bale	....
2	Bare	....	**12**	Sale	....
3	Fair	....	**13**	Ale	....
4	Hair	....	**14**	Tale	....
5	Tea	....	**15**	Vale	....
6	Pear	....	**16**	Whale	....
7	Dear	....	**17**	Which	....
8	For	....	**18**	Pale	....
9	Bate	....	**19**	War	....
10	Fate	....	**20**	Sun	....

20. Homophones again

In this exercise you are presented with a list of words again. You are required to find another word that sounds the same but is spelt differently and has a different meaning.

1	Male	....	**11**	Not	....
2	Two	....	**12**	Queue	....
3	Sew	....	**13**	Leak	....
4	Hole	....	**14**	Feet	....
5	Flare	....	**15**	Beat	....
6	Dough	....	**16**	Bore	....
7	Key	....	**17**	Bored	....
8	Plain	....	**18**	You	....
9	Check	....	**19**	Sweet	....
10	Fur	....	**20**	Tire	....

21. Synonyms

These are words that are spelt differently and sound different but have similar meanings.

In this exercise you are required to match words that have similar meanings, from column 1 with those in column 2. In column 3 you should write the word from column 1 that has the similar meaning with the word in column 2.

Try these and see if you can do them in less than **three** minutes.

The first one has been done for you!

	Column 1	Column 2	Column 3
1	Fight	Nearby	Close
2	Sea	Climb	
3	Friend	Absolute	
4	Enemy	Foreign	
5	Far	Abuse	
6	Concept	Distant	
7	Abduct	Ocean	
8	Complete	Arbiter	
9	Misuse	Mate	
10	Alien	Aroma	
11	Similar	Brawl	
12	Judge	Foe	
13	Fragrance	Idea	
14	Ascend	Kidnap	
15	Close	Alike	
16	Audio	Behind	
17	Bandit	Benefit	
18	Rear	Garbage	
19	Advantage	Outlaw	
20	Rubbish	Sound	

22. More synonyms

In the following exercises you are again required to match words that have similar meanings, from column 1 with those in column 2. In column 3 you should write the word from column 1 that has the similar meaning with the word in column 2.

	Column 1	Column 2	Column 3
1	Garbage	Empty	
2	Gaol	Wound	
3	Blank	Least	
4	Latrine	Grab	
5	Present	Channel	
6	Close	Insect	
7	Fleer	Refuse	
8	Gash	Jail	
9	Smallest	Sham	
10	Seize	Drum	
11	Groove	Border	
12	Bug	Pester	
13	Bogus	Fragile	
14	Counter	Inferior	
15	Curd	Lavatory	
16	Crummy	Oppose	
17	Brittle	Sneer	
18	Bother	Shut	
19	Boundary	Gift	
20	Bongo	Cheese	

	Column 1	Column 2	Column 3
1	Mad	Rude	
2	Odour	Sailor	
3	Moisture	Foe	
4	Prohibit	Unite	
5	Broad	Fable	
6	Curb	Sharp	
7	Coarse	Weariness	
8	Conceal	Feeble	
9	Interior	Round	
10	Difficult	Dwelling	
11	Insolent	Insane	
12	Join	Smell	
13	Mariner	Dampness	
14	Enemy	Forbid	
15	Myth	Wide	
16	Acute	Control	
17	Fatigue	Rough	
18	Weak	Hide	
19	Circular	Inside	
20	Abode	Hard	

	Column 1	Column 2	Column 3
1	Buy	Peaceful	
2	Rank	Clear	
3	Rapid	Riches	
4	Remedy	Strict	
5	Reveal	Horse	
6	Sturdy	Slim	
7	Surrender	Position	
8	Sleek	Empty	
9	Suspend	Annually	
10	Tranquil	Defeat	
11	Steed	Anger	
12	Slender	Quick	
13	Futile	Purchase	
14	Vacant	Pointless	
15	Yearly	Cure	
16	Vanquish	Show	
17	Stern	Strong	
18	Wealth	Yield	
19	Wrath	Smooth	
20	Transparent	Hang	

23. Antonyms

These are words that have opposite meanings.

In this exercise you are required to find the word that has an opposite meaning from the box below and match it with the word in the list.

1 Opponent	**8** Low	**15** Rear
2 Hard	**9** Liquid	**16** Below
3 Bright	**10** Good	**17** Open
4 Dull	**11** Evil	**18** Shut
5 Foe	**12** Front	**19** Friend
6 Rigid	**13** Closed	**20** Tight
7 Bendable	**14** Right	

1   Flexible   *Answer* [ ]

2   Solid   *Answer* [ ]

3   Shiny   *Answer* [ ]

4   Enemy   *Answer* [ ]

5   High   *Answer* [ ]

6   Above   *Answer* [ ]

7   Back   *Answer* [ ]

8   Left   *Answer* [ ]

9   Shut   *Answer* [ ]

10   Bad   *Answer* [ ]

24. More antonyms

In this exercise you are again required to find the word that has an opposite meaning from the box below and match it with the word in the list.

1 Ample	**8** Fixed	**15** Flexible
2 Liquid	**9** Remove	**16** Rigid
3 Increase	**10** Understand	**17** First
4 Solid	**11** Discourage	**18** Vacant
5 Inspire	**12** Decrease	**19** Scarce
6 Full	**13** Singular	**20** Final
7 Replace	**14** Many	

1 Empty   *Answer* ☐

2 Last   *Answer* ☐

3 Fluid   *Answer* ☐

4 Increment   *Answer* ☐

5 Loose   *Answer* ☐

6 Motivate   *Answer* ☐

7 Extract   *Answer* ☐

8 Plural   *Answer* ☐

9 Pliable   *Answer* ☐

10 Plenty   *Answer* ☐

25. Creating compound words

In this exercise you are required to select two words from each row to create a new single word (a compound word).

For example: the words SUN and DAY can be combined to create a new single word SUNDAY.

See how many you can do in **five** minutes – time your self accurately.
Underline the two words that you think can form a new single word.

1	Sun	Moon	Day	Year	Pluto
2	He	She	Her	Art	Design
3	Motor	Train	Lorry	Car	Plane
4	Flip	Turn	Side	Arm	Mat
5	Even	After	Affray	Affirm	Noon
6	Allow	True	Able	Alpha	Alpine
7	Alpha	Race	Bet	Alms	Also
8	Amalgam	Alter	Always	Never	Ate
9	Anti	Month	Body	Hand	Leg
10	God	Anti	Heaven	Christ	Saint
11	Anti	Day	Month	Social	Year
12	Hear	Audio	Listen	Meter	Here
13	Car	Auto	Draw	Graph	Authority
14	Auto	Bend	Turn	Friend	Mate
15	Front	Back	Top	Hand	Toe
16	Back	Clock	Watch	Ache	Round
17	Desk	Back	Chair	Ward	Book
18	Bag	Scale	Pipe	Exercise	Hard
19	High	Height	Land	Ocean	Black
20	Lorry	Rail	Trail	Way	Freight
21	Base	Case	Fall	Ball	Tall
22	Bat	Cat	Ten	Seven	Ben
23	Do	Be	Never	Come	Proper
24	Bed	Chair	Dress	Clothes	Shoes
25	Pot	Bed	Hat	Pat	Pan

26. More compound words

In this exercise you are again required to select two words from each line to create a new single word (a compound word).

See how many you can do in **five** minutes. Underline the two words that you think can form a new single word.

1	Blind	Deaf	Day	Month	Date
2	Pot	Pan	Block	Hard	Age
3	Brother	Bother	All	Some	Sister
4	Top	Bottom	Under	More	Less
5	Foot	Hole	Blind	Sport	Spot
6	Flour	Bread	Butter	Crumb	Cheese
7	Slow	Broke	Break	Speed	Fast
8	Table	Blind	Beauty	Task	Fold
9	Bride	Woman	Man	Groom	Father
10	Brief	Face	Base	Case	Lace
11	Brunt	Brute	Fine	Back	Force
12	Break	Quick	Able	Speedily	Hard
13	Beads	Chain	Round	Saw	Seen
14	Sit	Chair	Table	Boy	Man
15	Chamber	Sleep	House	Maid	Paid
16	Grooms	Brides	Butler	Maid	Servant
17	Yellow	Colour	Full	Blind	Tense
18	Common	Sensor	Fever	Wealth	Poverty
19	Copy	Work	Right	Sight	Letter
20	Wheat	Corn	Solidly	Wall	Lightly
21	Counter	Shelf	Soil	Foil	Boil
22	Fall	Crash	Tumble	Over	Land
23	Charter	Scale	Counter	Taste	Balance
24	Band	Counter	Sand	Act	Display
25	Centre	Pull	Table	Chair	Spoon

27. Compound words again

Try this exercise again. See how many you can do in **five** minutes.
Underline the two words that you think can form a new single word.

1	Arms	Coat	Pattern	Hanger	Banger
2	Gear	Motor	Cane	Stick	Bus
3	Import	Export	Insect	Ant	Bee
4	Abroad	Home	Officer	Work	Factory
5	Honey	Sugar	Brush	Comb	Sweet
6	Hour	Day	Plastic	Glass	Paper
7	Male	Man	Female	Rude	Kind
8	Alive	Dead	String	Line	Foot
9	Snow	Ice	Milk	Cream	Butter
10	Sun	Honey	Earth	Sweeter	Moon
11	Honey	Lot	Dot	Pot	Bread
12	Bed	Fed	Like	Linen	Led
13	Beet	Beat	Foot	Cook	Root
14	Be	Root	Hold	Bold	Sold
15	Birth	Death	Year	Month	Day
16	White	Black	Toe	Head	Mouth
17	Church	Temple	Warden	Police	Guest
18	School	Class	More	Less	Greater
19	Cloak	Tower	Person	Room	Tier
20	Simple	Grand	People	Fun	Father
21	Coast	Sea	Boat	Guard	Soldier
22	Hat	Fat	Him	Her	Them
23	Game	Sport	Keeper	Find	Giver
24	Flat	Plat	Born	Form	From
25	Cat	Sat	Pot	Urn	Ten

28. Four-minute compound words

See how many you can do in **four** minutes. Underline the two words that you think can form a new single word.

1	Bread	Broad	Cost	Cast	Frost
2	Brother	Uncle	Hood	Rude	Food
3	Thump	Bump	Sister	Father	Kin
4	Bus	Train	Queen	King	Lorry
5	Tap	Cap	Rat	Able	Kane
6	Care	Mare	More	Less	Great
7	Car	Van	Pot	Rot	Got
8	Check	Pit	Bore	Mate	Rate
9	Waste	Cart	Car	Pound	Ton
10	Thin	Wide	Broad	Road	Way
11	Common	Rare	Site	Place	Distance
12	Complain	Disagree	Pest	Bug	Ant
13	Rough	Gentle	Ghost	Man	Train
14	Ticket	Gate	Lost	Kiosk	Way
15	For	Four	Given	Taken	Miss
16	Bear	Fox	Rodent	Hound	Terrier
17	Fond	Taste	Ant	Hate	Twist
18	Dream	Hear	Foot	Hurt	Steps
19	Eye	Nose	Hair	Brow	Brown
20	Feat	Them	Her	Escape	Hands
21	Cloth	Fabric	Tempt	Ate	Past
22	Mate	Friend	Boat	Liner	Ship
23	Foot	Leg	Sky	Path	Ground
24	Sport	Game	Play	Ball	Keeper
25	Cool	Warm	Ant	Freeze	Spider

29. Three-minute compound words

See how many you can do in **three** minutes. Underline the two words that you think can form a new single word.

1	Fruit	Vegetable	Greater	Less	Given
2	Lost	Gain	Half	Fully	Empty
3	Doctor	For	Against	Ward	Board
4	Four	Number	Lots	Some	Many
5	Frame	Around	Work	Idol	Hardly
6	Estate	Land	Guard	Train	Mark
7	Eye	Face	Pan	Cook	Lid
8	Travel	Fare	Country	Home	Well
9	Cot	Bed	Weight	Pound	Ton
10	Front	Feed	Male	Person	Back
11	For	Against	Play	Tune	Sing
12	Grate	Gate	Door	Crash	Accident
13	Plane	Fly	Bug	Wheel	Under
14	God	Heaven	Boy	Hell	Son
15	Against	For	Young	Age	Male
16	Dark	Day	Flash	Front	Back
17	Dart	Arrow	Mouth	Face	Spear
18	Body	Eye	Wet	Sight	Truth
19	Under	Over	Metal	Mine	Your
20	Count	Numbers	Many	Less	Over
21	Good	Kind	Estate	Will	Lord
22	Large	Grand	Run	Sit	Stand
23	Plane	Fly	Twist	Over	Truth
24	Post	Counter	Holder	Part	Spares
25	Foot	Twister	Hold	Break	Gone

30. Analogies

1 Cat is to mouse as spider is to:

A. web   B. fly   C. scorpion   D. bathroom

Answer [   ]

2 Cat is to kitten as dog is to:

A. canine   B. labrador   C. pup   D. Fido

Answer [   ]

3 One is to single as two is to:

A. many   B. three   C. more   D. couple

Answer [   ]

4 Wing is to bird as fin is to:

A. duck   B. fish   C. heron   D. flamingo

Answer [   ]

5 Father is to son as mother is to:

A. daughter   B. sibling   C. female   D. women

Answer [   ]

6 January is to February as November is to:

A. October   B. December   C. September   D. August

Answer [   ]

7 Shell is to egg as rind is to:

A. apple   B. pear   C. orange   D. cherry

Answer [   ]

8 Water is to pipes as electricity is to:

A. generators   B. pylons   C. wires   D. switch

Answer [   ]

9 Tree is to forest as sheep is to:

    A. herd   B. gaggle   C. pack   D. flock

                Answer

10 Left is to right as west is to:

    A. east   B. west   C. north   D. south

                Answer

11 Early is to late as stop is to:

    A. halt   B. commence   C. refrain   D. complete

                Answer

12 Centimetres is to metre as inches is to:

    A. foot   B. yard   C. fathom   D. mile

                Answer

13 Radio is to listen as book is to:

    A. look   B. peruse   C. encode   D. comprehensive

                Answer

14 Vicar is to church as curator is to:

    A. museum   B. school   C. temple   D. station

                Answer

15 Pilot is to aeroplane as driver is to:

    A. automobile   B. spaceship   C. ship   D. horse

                Answer

16 Elephant is to herd as lion is to:

    A. flock   B. pack   C. herd   D. pride

                Answer

17   Wolf is to pack as locust is to:

A. herd   B. plague   C. bevy   D. crew

Answer [   ]

18   Cattle is to herd as monkey is to:

A. team   B. tribe   C. troop   D. gang

Answer [   ]

19   Bird is to flock as whale is to:

A. school   B. shoal   C. band   D. gang

Answer [   ]

20   Sailor is to crew as dancer is to:

A. gaggle   B. troupe   C. host   D. choir

Answer [   ]

21   Tree is to forest as book is to:

A. shelf   B. reader   C. library   D. pulp

Answer [   ]

22   Banana is to bunch as leopard is to:

A. pride   B. leap   C. nest   D. pace

Answer [   ]

23   Audience is to concert as congregation is to:

A. riot   B. street   C. mass   D. football match

Answer [   ]

24   Dozen is to twelve as couple is to:

A. one   B. two   C. three   D. four

Answer [   ]

25 Cat is to kitten as eel is to:

A. eel   B. eeler   C. elver   D. elder

Answer ⬚

Numerical tests

Work through the following examples at your own pace. You will find they become progressively harder and time limits are suggested for some of the material. The severity of the timed exercises are comparable to what you will face in real tests at the intermediate level.

This section is divided into two parts. The first provides practice in the all important skills of approximation, the second consists of practice questions in numerical reasoning.

Do not use a calculator except to check your answers. There is not space here to show you how to do these calculations. If you are unable to do some of them, ask a friend to show you. Alternatively, your local library will have books that demonstrate how to do these sums together with further practice examples.

Some tests set out to measure your skills in approximating the answer to calculations. Even if you do not have to face such a test, it is a useful skill to develop as it can lead to your being far quicker in many types of numerical test, and can also help to keep a check on calculations performed on a calculator.

To help you develop this skill we have provided you with estimating exercises for each of the four rules and for fractions and percentages. Estimating is very useful in the case of multiple-choice numerical tests.

When you approximate, do not work the sum out; instead, use your knowledge of the relationship between numbers to make an educated guess at the answer. Round up numbers to the nearest convenient figure and look at the suggested answers for the nearest to your estimate.

This section is divided into two parts: the first offers exercises in approximating and the second consists of practical numerical problems, entitled numerical reasoning.

1. Approximating

Rounding off numbers (1)

The purpose of this exercise is to help you make rough calculations quickly. This is particularly useful when you are presented with several answers and you have to choose one of them. By rounding off numbers and then doing the calculations you will have an answer that will be near enough to the correct answer.

First, we will ask you to round off to the nearest whole number. Later you will have the opportunity to do some calculations.

Now try the following.

Example: 2.89 is nearest to 3

1	99.99	is nearest to ....
2	9.9	is nearest to ....
3	1.89	is nearest to ....
4	9.19	is nearest to ....
5	7.8	is nearest to ....
6	499.67	is nearest to ....
7	115.10	is nearest to ....
8	5.8892	is nearest to ....
9	3.12	is nearest to ....
10	6.2113	is nearest to ....
11	2.102	is nearest to ....
12	8.421	is nearest to ....
13	5.6110	is nearest to ....
14	7.9876	is nearest to ....
15	44.898	is nearest to ....

Rounding off numbers (2)

In this exercise you have to convert the figures to the nearest convenient sum.

Example:
95% of 487 would become 100% of 500
29% of 291 would become 30% of 300

1   19% of 694 ....

2   87% of 55 ....

3   52% of 59 ....

4   20% of 987 ....

5   47% of 188 ....

6   18% of 94 ....

7   192% of 106 ....

8   9% of 888 ....

9   52% of 805 ....

10 43% of 82 ....

11 8.9% of 39.8 ....

12 4.99% of 47.989 ....

13 4.965% of 98.932 ....

14 119.5% of 999.659 ....

15 9.98% of 699 ....

Rounding off numbers (3)

In this exercise you should first round off the numbers before making
the calculations, giving your answers in nearest whole numbers.

Example:

Add	6.983	is nearest to	7
	3.896	is nearest to	4
	1.883	is nearest to	2
Answer			13

Now try the following. Remember we only need the nearest answer,
not the exact one.

1 Add   5.8892
3.12
6.2113   *Answer* [　　　　　]

2 Add   449.67
99.99
1.89   *Answer* [　　　　　]

3 Subtract   9.9
1.89   *Answer* [　　　　　]

4 Subtract   499.67
199.76   *Answer* [　　　　　]

5 Multiply   99.68
1.95   *Answer* [　　　　　]

6 Multiply   6969.763
1.996   *Answer* [　　　　　]

7 Divide 6969.763 by 1.996

Answer [　　　　　]

8 Divide 7998.687 by 3.893

Answer [　　　　　]

9 What is 10% of 9.99?

Answer [　　　　　]

10 What is 20% of 9.99?

Answer [　　　　　]

11 3.321 + 4.1 + 10.1

Answer [　　　　　]

12   699.76 + 99.89

Answer [   ]

13   699.76 − 99.89

Answer [   ]

14   9.9% of 49.789

Answer [   ]

15   49.9% of 9.9

Answer [   ]

Addition

In this exercise you should approximate the answers as quickly as you can and then choose an answer from the box.

1   0.49 + 399 + 49 =

Answer [   ]

2   3098 + 2056 + 1078 =

Answer [   ]

3   749 + 249 =

Answer [   ]

4   2258.3 + 4934.1 + 5.2 =

Answer [   ]

5   14.78 + 20.096 + 16.04 + 50 =

Answer [   ]

6   1.5 + 59 + 39 + 50.5 =

Answer [   ]

7 $0.5 + 4.5 + 0.5 + 500.5 =$

Answer

8 $509 + 309 + 209 + 203 =$

Answer

9 $5035 + 6035 + 4030 =$

Answer

10 $1559 + 2539 + 3332 =$

Answer

7430	1230	15100
7709	448.49	6232
150	506	998
7197.6	100.916	200.919

Subtraction

Estimate the following:

You will be able to identify the correct answers far more quickly if you estimate rather than work out the calculations fully, round up figures to convenient sums, and look for the exact answers among those suggested in the box.

1 $139 - 17 =$

Answer

2 $759 - 732 =$

Answer

3 $9.87 - 7.95 =$

Answer

4   2987 − 499 =

Answer [   ]

5   13.07 − 2.85 =

Answer [   ]

6   634 − 171 =

Answer [   ]

7   6278 − 1483 =

Answer [   ]

8   555 − 326 =

Answer [   ]

9   9987 − 399.12 =

Answer [   ]

10   99.45 − 25.60 =

Answer [   ]

10.22	73.85	122
4795	27	1.92
463	9587.88	229
2488		

Multiplication

In this exercise you should approximate the answers as quickly as you can and then choose an answer from the box.

1   59 × 5 × 5 =

Answer [   ]

2 $78 \times 10 \times 19 =$

Answer [　　　　　]

3 $2.5 \times 10 \times 5 =$

Answer [　　　　　]

4 $55 \times 3 \times 10 =$

Answer [　　　　　]

5 $500 \times 0.5 \times 10 =$

Answer [　　　　　]

6 $55 \times 6 \times 0.5 =$

Answer [　　　　　]

7 $100 \times 100 \times 1 =$

Answer [　　　　　]

8 $200 \times 100 \times 1.5 =$

Answer [　　　　　]

9 $100 \times 0.9999 =$

Answer [　　　　　]

10 $100 \times 0.5 \times 0.999 =$

Answer [　　　　　]

49.95	99.99	225
30000	335	10000
445	165	2500
1650	555	125
14820	1475	665

Division

Estimate the following and choose an answer from the box:

1 $3 \overline{)24.6}$ *Answer* [　　　　　]

2 $9 \overline{)198}$ *Answer* [　　　　　]

3 $596 \overline{)1072.8}$ *Answer* [　　　　　]

4 $4.5 \overline{)495}$ *Answer* [　　　　　]

5 $9.9 \overline{)9801}$ *Answer* [　　　　　]

| 110 | 990 | 8.2 | 22 | 1.8 |

Percentages

In this exercise you should approximate the answers as quickly as you can and then choose an answer from the box.

1 10% of 500 =   *Answer* [　　　　　]

2 20% of 600 =   *Answer* [　　　　　]

3 33% of 999 =   *Answer* [　　　　　]

4 49% of 749 =   *Answer* [　　　　　]

5 5% of 5000 =   *Answer* [　　　　　]

6 29% of 695 =   *Answer* [　　　　　]

7 18% of 95.99 =   *Answer* [　　　　　]

8 16% of 450 =   *Answer* [　　　　　]

9 11% of 19000 =   *Answer* [ ]

10 9% of 5000 =   *Answer* [ ]

250	450	645
2090	750	201.55
855	17.28	72
50	367.01	960
329.67	540	120

Fractions

Estimate the following and choose an answer from the box:

1 $\frac{1}{4}$ of 55 =   *Answer* [ ]

2 $\frac{1}{3}$ of 24 =   *Answer* [ ]

3 $\frac{2}{3}$ of 90 =   *Answer* [ ]

4 $\frac{1}{4}$ of 124 =   *Answer* [ ]

5 $\frac{1}{2} + \frac{2}{3} + 1\frac{1}{4}$ =   *Answer* [ ]

8	60	$2\frac{1}{12}$	$13\frac{3}{4}$	31

Mixed

In this exercise you should approximate the answers. You should do this by rounding off the numbers and then roughly calculating the answer. Once you have done this, pick the correct answer from the box.

Now do these 12 questions in **five** minutes.

1 29 + 41 + 29   *Answer* [ ]

2 99 − 19   *Answer* [ ]

3 19% of 49 *Answer* [ ]

4 9 × 18 *Answer* [ ]

5 395 ÷ 9 *Answer* [ ]

6 0.9 + 89.1 − 14.6 *Answer* [ ]

7 37% of 385 *Answer* [ ]

8 845 ÷ 12 *Answer* [ ]

9 456
654
+123 *Answer* [ ]

10 5678
−4567 *Answer* [ ]

11 456
×12 *Answer* [ ]

12 20 = X% of 400 What is X?

Answer [ ]

55	20	195
68	111	1111
1233	70.41	142.45
75.4	43.88	162
9.31	80	99
5472	4527	5

More percentages and some essential ratios

Try these further examples. Being confident, fast and accurate in these essential operations is key to success in psychometric tests today. So keep practising without a calculator. Explanations and answers are provided on page 000. If the percentage is reoccurring then work it to only one decimal place.

Changing fractions to percentages

Tip: To change a fraction to a percentage divide 100 by the bottom value and then multiply the outcome by the top value.

1   Find $\frac{1}{2}$ as a percentage.   *Answer*   [   ]

2   Find $\frac{1}{4}$ as a percentage.   *Answer*   [   ]

3   Find $\frac{1}{3}$ as a percentage.   *Answer*   [   ]

4   Find $\frac{1}{5}$ as a percentage.   *Answer*   [   ]

5   Find $\frac{1}{8}$ as a percentage.   *Answer*   [   ]

6   Find $\frac{1}{16}$ as a percentage.   *Answer*   [   ]

7   Find $\frac{1}{12}$ as a percentage.   *Answer*   [   ]

8   Find $\frac{1}{9}$ as a percentage.   *Answer*   [   ]

9   Find $\frac{2}{3}$ as a percentage.   *Answer*   [   ]

10   Find $\frac{3}{5}$ as a percentage.   *Answer*   [   ]

11   Find $\frac{6}{16}$ as a percentage.   *Answer*   [   ]

12   Find $\frac{5}{8}$ as a percentage.   *Answer*   [   ]

Changing between decimals and percentages

Tip: Simply multiply a decimal by 100 to get the equivalent percentage and divide the percentage by 100 to get the equivalent decimal.

1   Convert 0.5 to a percentage.   *Answer*   ☐

2   Convert 0.2 to a percentage   *Answer*   ☐

3   Convert 0.6 to a percentage.   *Answer*   ☐

4   Convert 0.4 to a percentage.   *Answer*   ☐

5   Convert 0.35 to a percentage.   *Answer*   ☐

6   Convert 0.72 to a percentage.   *Answer*   ☐

7   Convert 0.425 to a percentage.   *Answer*   ☐

8   Convert 0.333 to a percentage.   *Answer*   ☐

9   Convert 0.5325 to a percentage.   *Answer*   ☐

10 Convert 25% to a decimal.   *Answer*   ☐

11 Convert 90% to a decimal.   *Answer*   ☐

12 Convert 5% to a decimal.   *Answer*   ☐

13 Convert 15% to a decimal.   *Answer*   ☐

14 Convert 2.4% to a decimal.   *Answer*   ☐

15 Convert 0.6% to a decimal.   *Answer*   ☐

A value expressed as a percentage of another

Tip: Write the first value as a percentage of the second and then convert the fraction into a percentage.

1   Find 15 as a percentage of 50.   *Answer* [   ]

2   Find 3 as a percentage of 25.   *Answer* [   ]

3   Find 5 as a percentage of 40.   *Answer* [   ]

4   Find 1 as a percentage of 5.   *Answer* [   ]

5   Find 6 as a percentage of 75.   *Answer* [   ]

6   Find 10 as a percentage of 12.5.   *Answer* [   ]

7   Find 2 as a percentage of 16.   *Answer* [   ]

8   Find 4 as a percentage of 80.   *Answer* [   ]

9   Find 12 as a percentage of 40.   *Answer* [   ]

10 Find 28 as a percentage of 70.   *Answer* [   ]

Finding percentages of quantities

Tip: Convert the percentage to a decimal and then multiply it by the quantity but be careful of the units.

1   Find 40% of £80.   *Answer* [   ]

2   Find 25% of 3 hours.   *Answer* [   ]

3   Find 15% of 40 metres.   *Answer* [   ]

4   Find 20% of £9.   *Answer* [   ]

5 Find 5% of 12 metres.   *Answer*

6 Find 10% of 12 hours.   *Answer*

7 Find 15% of £520.   *Answer*

8 Find 30% of 1 hour 30 minutes.   *Answer*

9 Find 20% of 18.3 metres.   *Answer*

10 Find 17.5% of 5 hours.   *Answer*

Percentage increase

Tip: Percentage increase is calculated by dividing the increase by the original amount and multiplying the answer by 100.

1 What is the percentage increase between 20 and 30?

Answer

2 What is the percentage increase between 40 and 48?

Answer

3 What is the percentage increase between 18 and 24?

Answer

4 What is the percentage increase between 80 and 112?

Answer

5 What is the percentage increase between 11 and 17.6?

Answer

6 What is the percentage increase between 25 and 32.5?

Answer

7   What is the percentage increase between 90 and 97.2?

Answer [   ]

8   What is the percentage increase between 8 and 9?

Answer [   ]

9   What is the percentage increase between 120 and 124.8?

Answer [   ]

10   What is the percentage increase between 36 and 57.6?

Answer [   ]

Percentage decrease

Tip: Work out percentage decrease by dividing the amount of decrease by the original amount and multiplying the answer by 100.

1   What is the percentage decrease between 100 and 95?

Answer [   ]

2   What is the percentage decrease between 50 and 42?

Answer [   ]

3   What is the percentage decrease between 75 and 57?

Answer [   ]

4   What is the percentage decrease between 80 and 44?

Answer [   ]

5   What is the percentage decrease between 120 and 48?

Answer [   ]

6   What is the percentage decrease between 8 and 2?

Answer [   ]

7 What is the percentage decrease between 90 and 9?

Answer [ ]

8 What is the percentage decrease between 25 and 17.5?

Answer [ ]

9 What is the percentage decrease between 30 and 26.4?

Answer [ ]

10 What is the percentage decrease between 65 and 50.7?

Answer [ ]

Percentage profit or loss

Tip: To calculate the percentage profit divide the amount of profit by the buying price and multiply the answer by 100; to calculate the percentage loss divide the loss by the buying price and multiply the answer by 100. Don't forget to state whether the answer is a profit or loss.

1 What is the percentage profit or loss if the buying price of an item was £10 and the selling price was £12?

Answer [ ]

2 What is the percentage profit or loss if the buying price of an item was £40 and the selling price was £32?

Answer [ ]

3 What is the percentage profit or loss if the buying price of an item was £50 and the selling price was £70?

Answer [ ]

4 What is the percentage profit or loss if the buying price of an item was £8 and the selling price was £7?

Answer

5 What is the percentage profit or loss if the buying price of an item was £25 and the selling price was £32.50?

Answer

6 What is the percentage profit or loss if the buying price of an item was £12 and the selling price was £2.40?

Answer

7 What is the percentage profit or loss if the buying price of an item was £5 and the selling price was £5.75?

Answer

8 What is the percentage profit or loss if the buying price of an item was £45 and the selling price was £13.50?

Answer

9 What is the percentage profit or loss if the buying price of an item was £70 and the selling price was £112?

Answer

10 What is the percentage profit or loss if the buying price of an item was £6.50 and the selling price was £6.11?

Answer

Ratios

Tip: To divide a sum by a ratio add together all the parts of the ratio, divide the amount by the answer; this gives you the value of each part, then calculate each share by multiplying the value of each part by the number of parts.

1 Divide 100 into the ratio 4 : 1.   *Answer* [ ]

2 Divide 49 into the ratio 3 : 4.   *Answer* [ ]

3 Divide 36 into the ratio 1 : 5.   *Answer* [ ]

4 Divide 72 into the ratio 5 : 3.   *Answer* [ ]

5 Divide 55 into the ratio 3 : 2.   *Answer* [ ]

6 Divide 130 into the ratio 1 : 7 : 2.   *Answer* [ ]

7 Divide 52 into the ratio 6 : 4 : 3.   *Answer* [ ]

8 Divide 55 into the ratio 7 : 3 : 12.   *Answer* [ ]

9 Divide 28 into the ratio 1 : 4 : 3.   *Answer* [ ]

10 Divide 60.5 into the ratio 2 : 5 : 4.   *Answer* [ ]

2. Numerical reasoning

Work these out without the use of a calculator.

1 Twenty-seven people are asked to contribute 50 pence each towards the cost of a leaving present for a colleague but three decline; how much is collected?

Answer [ ]

2 Your telephone bill comprises a standing charge of £7.93, £40.47 worth of calls and £7.26 of value added tax. What is the total?

Answer [ ]

3 Nicky works flexitime and is contracted to work a 35-hour week. For three weeks she has only worked 27½ hours a week. How many hours does she owe?

Answer [   ]

Work towards getting this sort of sum right consistently and quickly.

4 A large company employs 15 per cent of the working population in a small town. The total population of the town is 70,000, of which 50 per cent is the working population. How many people are employed by the company?

Answer [   ]

5 A shop sells washing machines for £150 plus VAT at 17.5 per cent. What is the total price that customers would have to pay?

Answer [   ]

6 The same shop has a special offer on a video and television when bought together. The combined price is £650 inclusive, less a discount of 12 per cent. What is the special offer price?

Answer [   ]

7 A clerical officer earns £12,000 gross per year. She is entitled to a tax-free personal allowance of £3,000 and pays income tax at 25 per cent on the balance. What is her net pay per year?

Answer [   ]

8 A senior clerical officer earns £15,000 gross per year. What is the annual net pay, assuming all the other information is as above?

Answer [   ]

9 A businessperson buys 500 pairs of shoes at a cost of £5,000. He wants to make a 30 per cent profit. What is the price he should charge for a pair of shoes?

Answer [   ]

10a A woman buys a television for £550, a CD player for £450 and a computer for £850. She gets a 10 per cent discount from the total price. How much has she paid?

Answer [   ]

10b If her two sons contribute two-thirds of the total cost, what would be the woman's share of the cost?

Answer [   ]

11 If Michael has £50, Chris has 50 per cent more than Michael, and Betty has only half as much as Chris, how much money does Betty have?

Answer [   ]

12 An employer has 60 people working for her and she wants to give a 15 per cent bonus to all her staff. How much extra would each staff member receive if the total weekly wage bill is normally £15,000?

Answer [   ]

13 How much extra would each staff member receive if the bonus is reduced to 10 per cent?

Answer [   ]

14 Claire earns £430.60 per week but £86.12 income tax and £43.60 National Insurance contributions are deducted. How much net pay does she receive?

Answer [   ]

Attempt the following 10 questions under realistic test conditions.

Allow yourself 10 minutes to complete them and do not use a calculator.

Do not turn the page until you are ready to begin.

1   A restaurant bill totals £42.80 and is to be divided between four people. How much has each person to pay?

Answer [   ]

2   How much value added tax, charged at 17.5 per cent, would be added to a pre-tax total of £88?

Answer [   ]

3   If a 2 kilowatt electric fire costs 10.7 pence an hour to run, how much would it cost to operate a 1 kilowatt fire for 16 hours?

Answer [   ]

Your speed and accuracy at this sort of calculation will greatly improve with practice.

4   If an academic gets 8 weeks a year study leave and 5 weeks holiday what percentage of the year does this represent?

Answer [   ]

5   A quarter of 180 houses are reserved for workers in essential services and a further $^2/_5$ are designated for homeless families. The rest are to be sold on the open market. How many are to be put up for sale?

Answer [   ]

6   If the fulfilment time for an order worsens from 5 days to 7.25 days, what is this increase in percentage terms?

Answer [   ]

7   If you can buy a 300g jar of chocolate spread for $3.60 or a 1kg jar for $12, which purchase represents the best value?

Answer [   ]

8   If the success rate in submitted proposals fell from 12 in 60 by three quarters, how many would you expect to succeed if you were to submit 40 further proposals?

Answer

9   Fifty pencils cost $16 and six trays of eggs containing 132 eggs cost $48. How much would 70 pencils and 22 eggs cost?

Answer

10   A population has increased by 4.5 per cent to 203,775. What was the original population?

Answer

Foreign currency exchange rates

Here is a table of different foreign currencies. The values shown are equal to £1 sterling. For example: £1 = 10 francs. (We are aware that many of these currencies no longer exist.)

French francs	10
Dutch guilders	5
Italian lire	2,500
German marks	3
US dollars	1.80
Indian rupees	65

Use the above exchange rates to calculate the following:

1   A customer wishes to purchase 390 German marks. How many pounds will she have to pay?

A. 390   B. 230   C. 190   D. 130   E. None of these

Answer

2 How many Indian rupees can you get for £350?

A. 600   B. 6,500   C. 7,500   D. 5,650   E. None of these

Answer [ ]

3 How many pounds would you get for 126 francs?

A. 10   B. 15   C. 12.60   D. 10.50   E. None of these

Answer [ ]

4 What are 500 guilders worth in German marks?

A. 100   B. 200   C. 300   D. 400   E. None of these

Answer [ ]

5 Convert 250,000 lire into Indian rupees. How many rupees is that?

A. 1,250   B. 6,500   C. 2,500   D. 100   E. None of these

Answer [ ]

6 If you bought 90 US dollars and 600 French francs, how many pounds would you require?

A. 250   B. 150   C. 125   D. 110   E. None of these

Answer [ ]

7 A tourist has £500 with which he intends to purchase some foreign currencies. He decides to buy francs for 25% of the pounds, marks for a further 25% and with the remaining 50% of the pounds he decides to buy Italian lire. What are the different amounts of currencies that the tourist will get?

	A.	B.	C.	D.	E.
francs	1,600	1,300	1,400	1,250	None
marks	375	475	275	375	of
lire	625,000	635,000	625,000	625,000	these

Answer [ ]

8 A woman returning from a holiday finds that she still has some foreign money left. She has 300 Dutch guilders, 500 US dollars and 50 francs in change, which she is not able to exchange. What is the total amount of pounds she will get?

A. 377.78   B. 337.78   C. 327.78
D. 347.78   E. None of these

Answer [   ]

9 A French tourist wishes to buy 850 dollars. How many francs will that cost him?

A. 7,566.67   B. 5,056.67   C. 4,722.22
D. 6,666.67   E. None of these

Answer [   ]

10 An American brings 7,200 dollars with her to London and wants to exchange them for pounds. How many pounds would she get after paying a 10% commission charge?

A. 2,600   B. 3,600   C. 4,600
D. 5,600   E. None of these

Answer [   ]

Clerical tests

These exercises will help in your preparation for the types of selection test that companies use to assess your suitability for clerical work and work with computers.

1. Coded instructions

These involve sets of rules or tables of information that you interpret and then apply to a series of situations or refer to in order to answer a series of questions.

Exercise 1

Establish from the table the answers to the questions.

Time	What happened	Where we were
9 am	the telephone rang	out shopping
12.00	the post arrived	watching the news on TV
1 pm	I paid the milk bill	on the doorstep
2 pm	did the washing	down the launderette
4 pm	cooked dinner	in the kitchen

Questions

1   Where was I at 2 pm? ....

2   What was I doing at 12.00? ....

3   What time was it when I was watching TV? ....

4   What was I doing while on the doorstep? ....

5   When did the post arrive? ....

6   What time did the phone ring? ....

Exercise 2

In this exercise you are required to translate the English sentences into the code equivalents by referring to the dictionary.

Dictionary

call	=	ranch
Fido	=	Tratma
dog	=	lippgai
is	=	nitco
black	=	modod
the	=	udyne

Example:

Call Fido = Ranch Tratma

Questions

1   The dog is black. ....

2   Fido is the dog. ....

3   Call the black dog. ....

Now translate these coded sentences into English.

4   Tratma udyne lippgai. ....

5   Nitco Tratma modod? ....

6   Nitco udyne lippgai Tratma? ....

Exercise 3

Computerised accounts system for a building society

Codes

Current account	C
Share account	S
Fixed account	F
Loan account	L
The code for the type of account is followed by an account number and a code indicating whether the account is in credit or overdrawn.	
Account in credit	OC
Account overdrawn	OD

Example:

A fixed account number 00210 in credit = F00210OC

Answer the following questions by selecting one of the suggested answers A, B, C or D. Indicate your answer by writing either A, B, C or D in the answer box.

Questions

1   A current account number 3679830 in credit.

   A. S367830OC

   B. L3679830OC

   C. C3367983OOC

   D. C3679830OC   *Answer*

2   A share account number 2213730 overdrawn.

   A. L2213730OC

   B. S2213730OD

   C. F2213730OC

   D. C2213730OD   *Answer*

3   A loan account number 087231 in credit.

   A. C087231OD

   B. S087231OC

   C. L087231OD

   D. L087231OC   *Answer*

Timed coded instructions exercise

Over the page is a timed coded instructions exercise. Allow yourself **five** minutes to answer the five questions.

Do not turn the page until you are ready to do the timed exercise.

A computerised till in a shop

If payment is made by credit card it is coded CT.
Payment by cheque is coded CHQ.
For cash the code is CS.
If the amount is less than £50 the letter U follows the code.
If the amount is over £50 the letter O follows the code.
For all furniture items the number 1 follows the letter U or O.
Other goods are numbered 2.

Answer the following questions by selecting one of the suggested answers. Indicate your answer by writing A, B, C or D in the answer box.

Example:

A man buys a suit for £150 and pays by credit card.

A. CTO1
B. CTU1
C. CTO2
D. CTU2   *Answer*   C

1   A couple buy a dining table for £99 and pay cash.
A. CS
B. CHQ
C. CS2
D. CSO1   *Answer*

2   A woman buys a shirt for £25 and pays by cheque.
A. CHQ
B. CGQ1
C. CHQ2
D. CHQU2   *Answer*

3   A man buys a chair for £49.99 and pays by credit card.

A. CTO1

B. CTU1

C. CTO2

D. CSU2   *Answer*

4   A bed is bought for £250 cash.

A. CTQ1

B. CTU1

C. CTO2

D. CSO1   *Answer*

5   Someone writes a cheque out to the value of £199.95 in payment of a colour TV.

A. CTU2

B. CSO1

C. CQHU2

D. CHQO2   *Answer*

END OF EXERCISE

More examples of this type of question can be found in the Kogan Page title, *How to Pass Computer Selection Tests.*

Exercise 4

1   There are six friends and their ages are as follows – two are 14 years of age, another two are 15 and the last two are 16.

What is their average age?

                          Answer

2   A person going to work walks for five minutes, waits for a bus for three minutes and is on the bus for 10 minutes. A walk from the bus stop to the train station takes seven minutes. The train journey is 30 minutes and the walk to the office from the train station is another eight minutes.

How long does it take for the whole journey?

Answer

3   A man buys the following items from a greengrocer, 1 kilo of apples, 500 grams of bananas, 350 grams of oranges, 1½ kilos of potatoes and 250 grams of tomatoes.

What is the total weight of all these items?

Answer

4   Neha is six years younger than Raheel. Raheel is two years older than Adeel and Uzair. Simrun is four years old. The difference in age between Simrun and Adeel is seven years.

How old is Neha?

Answer

5   A box can hold 720 packets of sugar and there are 24 such boxes. What is the total number of packets?

Answer

6   A person buys seven items from a supermarket and the cost of these items is £10.50. What is the average price of each item?

Answer

7   An electrician has 8m of cable. If she uses 2.36m, how much will she have left?

Answer

8   Neha and Simrun have a combined weight of 141.50kg. If Simrun weighs 68.40kg, what is Neha's weight?

Answer

9 Raheel and Adeel have a combined height of 3.74m. Raheel is 24cm taller than Adeel. What are their respective heights?

Raheel   *Answer* [   ]

Adeel   *Answer* [   ]

10 Adam earns £15,450, John earns £ 14,250, Jamie earns £18,325 and Tom earns £19,175. Calculate the total and the average salary.

Total   *Answer* [   ]

Average   *Answer* [   ]

11 A computer operator is able to input 120 characters per minute using a standard keyboard. How many characters can be typed in half an hour?

                         Answer [   ]

12 A company employs 500 people, of whom 20 per cent are men. How many women work there?

                         Answer [   ]

13 If a computer model A costs £600, model B costs 50 per cent more than model A and model C costs half the price of model B, how much does model C cost?

                         Answer [   ]

14 A businessperson buys 20 computers at a cost of £10,000. He wants to make a 20 per cent profit on the computers. How much should he sell each computer at?

                         Answer [   ]

15 John gives three-quarters of his sweets to Julie, and Julie gives a third of this amount to Mike. If Mike receives nine sweets, how many sweets did John start with?

                         Answer [   ]

Exercise 5

In this exercise you are required to carry out calculations. However, instead of numbers you are presented with letters. Each letter is given a value, but your answer will be in number format.

Let: $A = 2$ $B = 3$ $C = 4$ $D = 5$

Example question:

$A + B = ?$

In this case the answer is 5 because $A = 2$ and $B = 3$, therefore $2 + 3 = 5$.

Remember that all calculations within brackets have to be carried out first.

Now work out the following:

1 $A + D =$ *Answer*

2 $(A + B) - B =$ *Answer*

3 $(B + D) \times A =$ *Answer*

4 $D - (A + B) =$ *Answer*

5 $(D \times B) - D =$ *Answer*

6 $A + B + C - D =$ *Answer*

7 $(D + C + B) \div A =$ *Answer*

8 $(C \times D) + (A \times B) =$ *Answer*

9 $(B \times C) - (A + C) =$ *Answer*

10 $B + C + D - A =$ *Answer*

Exercise 6

Let: $A = 5$ $B = 8$ $C = 14$ $D = 16$

1 $(B + C) \times A =$ *Answer*

2 $(C - B) \times D =$ *Answer*

3   (D – A) – (C – B) =   *Answer*   [   ]

4   (D – C) × (A + B) =   *Answer*   [   ]

Exercise 7

In this exercise you will be presented with numerical problems that are represented by letters. Each letter has been given a value that corresponds with its position in the alphabet. Thus 'A' =1 and 'Z' = 26.

Give your answers as letters.

Example question:

A + B = ?

A = 1 B = 2 C = 3 D = 4 etc. Therefore A(1) + B(2) = C(3)

Hint: You will find it helpful to write down the alphabet somewhere and to number each letter.

1   F + ? = P   *Answer*   [   ]

2   C + ? = J   *Answer*   [   ]

3   L + D = ?   *Answer*   [   ]

4   Z – B = ?   *Answer*   [   ]

5   ? × K = V   *Answer*   [   ]

6   C + D + ? = N   *Answer*   [   ]

7   R – H = ?   *Answer*   [   ]

8   P + A – G = ?   *Answer*   [   ]

9   V + W – Z = ?   *Answer*   [   ]

10   T × E / D = ?   *Answer*   [   ]

11   J × B / ? = A   *Answer*   [   ]

12   F × ? – J = Z   *Answer*   [   ]

13   Y + ? – T = Z   *Answer*   [   ]

14   R + P − L = ?   *Answer*   [ ]

15   (C + D) × ? = U   *Answer*   [ ]

For this part of the exercise please give the answers in numbers.

16   (P + N) × E = ?   *Answer*   [ ]

17   (Z / B) × L = ?   *Answer*   [ ]

18   V + H + R − T = ?   *Answer*   [ ]

19   (E × Y + Y) / B = ?   *Answer*   [ ]

20   T + (U / C) = ?   *Answer*   [ ]

Exercise 8

Constructing equations

In this exercise your task is to arrange the numbers and arithmetic symbols, presented below, to make true equations. You are then to choose a number from the list on the right that gives you a correct answer.

Symbols used are: Plus (+), Minus (−), Multiply (×) and Divide (/)

Example questions:

1   1 2 3 + −   A. 0   B. 3   C. 5   D. 6   E. 1

2   2 3 4 + ×   A. 20   B. 16   C. 12   D. 10   E. 8

The answers to the example questions are:

1   1 + 2 − 3 = 0   The answer is A.

We could have written the equation thus:

   3 + 2 − 1 = 4

However, this is not available in the answer list.

2   2 × 3 + 4 = 10   The answer is D.

NOW TRY THE FOLLOWING QUESTIONS

1 5 3 1 + −   A. 6   B. 5   C. 4   D. 3   E. 2

Answer

2 9 6 7 + −   A. 10 B. 11 C. 12 D. 6   E. 7

Answer

3 8 4 5 + −   A. 4   B. 5   C. 6   D. 7   E. 8

Answer

4 2 3 4 5 + + −   A. 3   B. 4   C. 5   D. 7   E. 9

Answer

5 6 1 8 9 + + −   A. 9   B. 10 C. 12 D. 14 E. 6

Answer

6 2 4 6 × −   A. 0   B. 18 C. 20 D. 10 E. 2

Answer

7 7 3 1 × −   A. 1   B. 3   C. 4   D. 7   E. 21

Answer

8 9 1 2 + +   A. 9   B. 10 C. 11 D. 12 E. 13

Answer

9 1 1 2 + −   A. 1   B. 5   C. 3   D. 2   E. 4

Answer

10 3 5 7 9 × + −   A. 17 B. 18 C. 28 D. 24 E. 60

Answer

Exercise 9

In this exercise you have to write the missing sign in the box so that the vertical and horizontal answers are equal. Look at the example below.

Example:

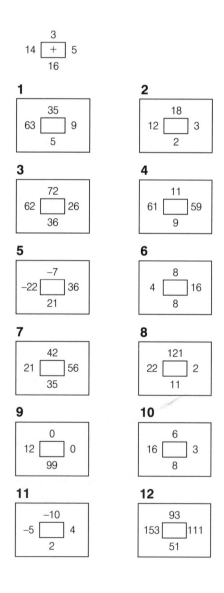

Exercise 10

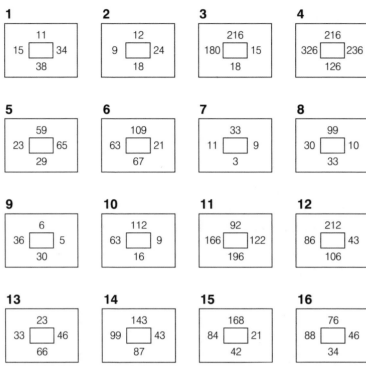

Exercise 11

1   If you were using a map with a scale of 5cm to 1km, how many
    kilometres would be represented by 75cm on the map?

   A. 5km

   B. 10km

   C. 15km

   D. 75km

   Answer [   ]

2   Tim and Tom are friends. They plan a trip to the seaside. They decide to hire a car for the day. The seaside is 79km from where they live. The cost of hiring the car is £45 plus 15p per km. How much will it cost them for the round trip?

A. £45.15

B. £58.70

C. £68.70

D. £90.30

Answer [   ]

3   They then decide to work out the amount of petrol they would need. The car will travel 15.5km on 1 litre of petrol. How much petrol will they need to the nearest whole litre?

A. 5 litres

B. 10 litres

C. 15 litres

D. 20 litres

Answer [   ]

4   Tim and Tom decide to have a party. They invited 80 people. But 10 per cent of them said they could not come. A quarter of all those who said they would come did not come. How many people came to the party?

A. 24

B. 38

C. 46

D. 54

Answer [   ]

5   Tim and Tom want to send a parcel of old clothes to a charity. They have four boxes to choose from. They want the box with the biggest volume. Which of these has the biggest volume?

A. 70cm × 55cm × 35cm

B. 70cm × 60cm × 30cm

C. 80cm × 60cm × 20cm

D. 80cm × 55cm × 20cm

Answer

A teacher asked the pupils in her tutor group to say how many hours they watched television per week. Once she had collected the data she then produced a chart to display the results. Use the chart to answer questions 6 to 9.

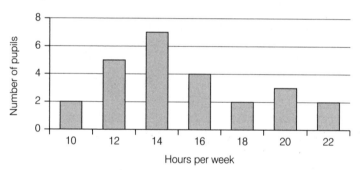

6   How many pupils are there in the class?

A. 7   B.   22

C. 25   D.   None of the above

Answer

7   What is the average time spent watching television (to the nearest hour)?

A. 4 hours   B.   6 hours

C. 14 hours   D.   16 hours

Answer

8 How many pupils watch 20 or more hours of television per week?

A. 2   B. 3
C. 4   D. 5

Answer [   ]

9 How many pupils watch television for under 16 hours per week?

A. 10   B. 12
C. 14   D. 16

Answer [   ]

The table below shows all the animals on a farm.

Use the information to answer questions 10 to 14.

Types of animal	Cows	Sheep	Pigs	Hens	Dogs	Horses
Number	30	90	60	25	3	2

10 How many cows, sheep and pigs does the farm have?

A. 160   B. 180
C. 260   D. 280

Answer [   ]

11 What fraction of the total number of animals on the farm are cows?

A. 1/5   B. 1/6
C. 1/7   D. 1/8

Answer [   ]

12 What is the ratio of cows to pigs?

A. 1:2   B. 1:3
C. 1:4   D. 1:5

Answer [   ]

13   What is the ratio of cows to sheep?

    A. 1 : 2   B. 1 : 3

    C. 1 : 4   D. 1 : 5

                         Answer [＿＿＿＿＿＿]

14   What is the ratio of horses to cows?

    A. 1:12   B. 1:13

    C. 1:14   D. 1:15

                         Answer [＿＿＿＿＿＿]

15   A new nursery is being opened. They plan to take in 40 children. The ratio of 1 : 4 is required. How many nursery teachers will they need?

    A. 5   B. 10

    C. 15   D. 20

                         Answer [＿＿＿＿＿＿]

A holiday guide has provided a table that shows the number of hours of sunshine on a Greek Island.

Use the table to answer questions 16 to 19 (you may need to find out the meaning of the following mathematical terms: mean, mode and median).

Month	Feb	Mar	April	May	June	July	Aug	Sept	Oct
Hours of sunshine – daily	6	7	8	9	11	12	10	9	9

16   What is the range of the daily hours of sunshine over the months shown?

    A. 5   B. 6

    C. 7   D. 8

                         Answer [＿＿＿＿＿＿]

17   What is the mean of the daily hours of sunshine for the months shown?

A. 7   B. 8

C. 9   D. 12

Answer [　　　　]

18   What is the median of the daily hours of sunshine for the months shown?

A. 7   B. 8

C. 9   D. 10

Answer [　　　　]

19   What is the mode of the daily hours of sunshine for the months shown?

A. 6   B. 7

C. 8   D. 9

Answer [　　　　]

20   Which of the following numbers is the biggest?

A. 1.067   B. 1.60

C. 1.67   D. 1.607

Answer [　　　　]

Exercise 12

In this exercise you are required to find the missing number from one of the boxes. The numbers are in some kind of a sequence, and it is your task to find that sequence in order to answer the question. The sequence may be horizontal or vertical.

1

1	?	5
2	4	6

A.1 B.2 C.3 D.4 E.5

Answer [　　　　]

2

2	?	8
16	32	64

A.6   B.4   C.3   D.5   E.10

Answer

3

3	9	27
?	243	729

A.61   B.90   C.81   D.101   E.141

Answer

4

6	12	?
48	96	192

A.18   B.20   C.22   D.24   E.36

Answer

5

2	20	15
4	?	30

A.10   B.40   C.8   D.16   E.18

Answer

6

5	15	30
?	75	105

A.45   B.70   C.50   D.65   E.60

Answer

7

1	6	12
19	27	?

A.35   B.40   C.46   D.36   E.34

Answer

8

1	6	15
3	9	?

A.19   B.20   C.21   D.27   E.30

Answer

9

3	12	27
7	17	?

A.37   B.36   C.34   D.33   E.31

Answer

10

?	15	45
1	3	9

A.3 B.4 C.5 D.6 E.7

Answer

Exercise 13

Put one of these mathematical signs (+ − × ÷) in each blank space to get the answer given. Some signs may be used more than once.

eg $12 + 9 \times 3 \div 7 = 9$

1 99 __ 3 __ 11 __ 18 = 26

2 25 __ 4 __ 20 __ 9 = 45

3 24 __ 3 __ 3 __ 3 = 25

4 40 __ 8 __ 3 __ 6 = 24

5 13 __ 3 __ 11 __ 3 = 150

6 15 __ 6 __ 10 __ 25 = 4

7 9 __ 5 __ 20 __ 4 = 70

8 15 __ 5 __ 8 __ 4 = 6

9 15 __ 3 __ 2 __ 30 = 3

10 19 __ 3 __ 2 __ 9 = 99

2. Flow diagrams

These exercises require you to interpret the information presented and use it to answer the questions.

Exercise 1. A catalogue order procedure

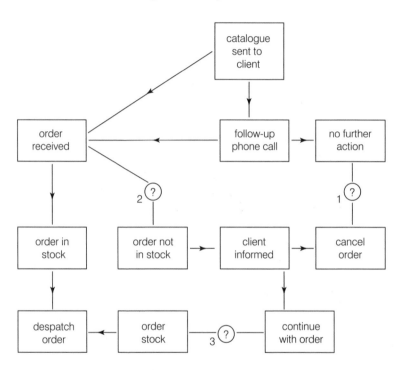

Study the flow diagram and decide which way the arrows ought to be drawn at points 1, 2 and 3. Indicate your answer by drawing arrows in the answer boxes provided.

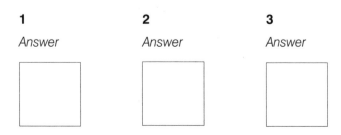

1

Answer

2

Answer

3

Answer

Exercise 2. A finance department's invoice system

Interpret the flow diagram and answer the questions.

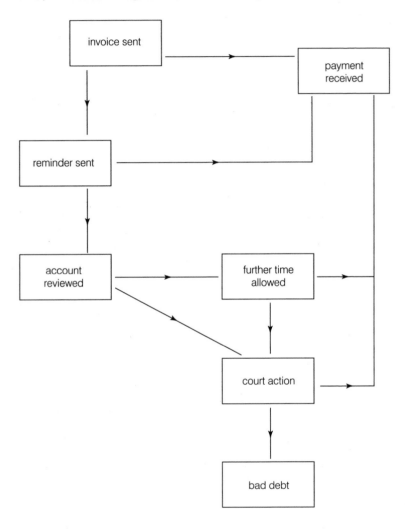

1   It was decided at the account review to give a customer extra time to pay but that time has now passed without result. What action should the accounts manager initiate?

Answer

_____

2   No payment has been received for an invoice. What action should be taken?

Answer

_____

3   If a reminder is sent after 30 days and the account review held after a further 30 days, what is the minimum period before court action is instigated?

Answer

_____

Timed flow diagram exercise

Over the page is a timed flow diagram exercise. Allow yourself **five** minutes to answer the five questions.

Do not turn the page until you are ready to do the timed exercise.

The recruitment process of a leading employer.

You have **five** minutes in which to study the flow diagram and answer the questions.

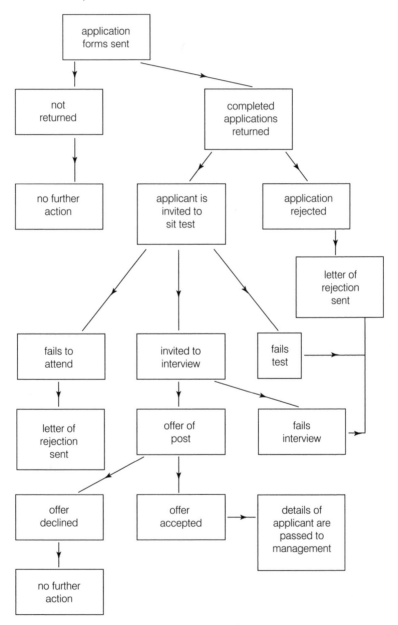

Indicate what the personnel officer should do if:

1   Someone fails to attend for interview.

   Answer

   _____

2   A candidate fails to return an application form.

   Answer

   _____

3   A candidate is successful at interview.

   Answer

   _____

4   A candidate submits a successful application form.

   Answer

   _____

5   A candidate accepts the offer of a post.

   Answer

   _____

END OF EXERCISE

3. Checking

In this exercise you are presented with a list of company names. On the left is the original list and on the right is a retyped version. Your task is to check the retyped version for any errors by comparing it with the original list on the left. Put brackets around the retyped version if there is an error.

Exercise 1

This exercise aims to assess your skills in checking speedily and accurately. Now complete this task in **three** minutes.

Original	Copy
Paine Chocolates	Pain Chocolates
Pall Mall Dispensing	Pall Mall Dispensing
Lodge Insurance Brokers	Lodge Insurence Brokers
Lodder Est Agts	LOdder Est Agts
Mill Hill Dry Clnrs	Mill Hill Dry Clnrs
Kahn Printers	Kahn Printers
Italian Piano Co	Italian Piano Co
Hoxtex Restaurants	Hoxtex Restaurant
Apollo Bed and Breakfast	Apollo Bedand Breakfast
Holloway Carpenters	Holloway Carpenters
Archway Halal Meat	Archway Hala Meat
Hookway Jewellers	Hookway Jewellers
Hi-tec School of Motoring	Hi-tec School of Motoring
Totland Hire Centre	Totland Hire Center
George's Recruitment	Georges Recruitment
West End Consultants	West End Consultants
Court Cars	Court cars
House of Lighting	Hourse of Lighting
Woxton Water Works	Woxton Water Works
Castletown Restaurants	Castletown Recruitments
Hardwood Doors Group Ltd	Hardwood Doors Group LTD
Mike's Do It Yourself Centre	Mike's Do It Yourself Centre
MITAKA Publishing House	MITAKA Publsihing House
Sunchung Takeaway	Sanchung Takeaway
Move Motorcycle Hire	Move Motorcyycle Hire
Portman Car and Van Rental	Portman Carr and Van Rental
Heitman and Son Accountants	Heitman and son Accountance
Ace Consulting Engineers	Ace Consulting Engineers
Hot Tandoori House	Hot Tundoori House
Safe Security Ltd	Safe security Ltd

Exercise 2

Original	*Copy*
ABC123	ABC123
ACCB/123/321	ACCB/123/321
CENTIMETRES/CUBIC	CENTEMETRES/CUBIC
GUMPTION	GUMPTION
MEASURES/CAPACITY	MAESURES/CAPACITY
987654321/123456789	987654321/123456789
987/123/654/456:	987/123/654/456
GERMANIUM-72.59	GERMANUM-72.59
MOLYBDENUM-95.94	MOLYBDENUM-95.94
NICKEL-58.71	NICKLE-58.71
ZIRCONIUM-91.22	ZIRCONIUM-91.22
PHOSPHORUS-30.9738	PHOSPHOROS-30.9738
MILLILITRES-36966	MILLILITERS-36966
MANGANESE-54.9380	MANGANESE-54.9380
DECAGRAMMES-15432	DECAGRAMMS-15432
KILOGRAMME-2205	KILOGRAMMES-2205
ANTIMONY-121.75	ANTIMONY-121.75
HYDROGEN-1.0080(H)	HYDROGIN-1.0080(H)
CHROMIUM-51.996	CHROMUIM-51.996
MINNESOTA STATE	MINNISOTA STATE
ZEDEKIAH	ZEDEKIAH
WYOMING/CHEYENNE	WYCOMING/CHEYENNE
TENNESSEE/NASHVILLE	TENESSEE/NASHVILLE
ZOROASTER	ZOROASTER
PENNSYLVANIA/H'BURG	PENNCYLVANIA/H'BURG
WHISTLER	WHISLER
VERSAILLES	VERSAILES
VERRUCOSE	VERRUCOSE
UNHALLOWED	UNIHALLOWED
TREACHEROUS	TREACHEROUS
TREASURY	TREASUERY
SPARE-PART	SPAIRE-PART
ROUSSEAU	RUOSSEAU
EQUIVALENTS	EQIUVALENTS
FLOUNCE	FLUONCE
HARDENBERG	HARDENBERG

Exercise 3

Original	*Copy*
123/456/789/AC	123/456/789/AC
987/654/321/CA	987/654/321/CA
32323/452/CIC	32332/452/CIC
ACEG/818/658	ACEG/818/658
BDFH/4653/12	BDFH/4653/12
ZED/678/TLT/010	ZED/678/TLT/010
WORLD/VIEW/83	WORLD/VEIW/83
ZEBEDEE/F/JJ	ZEBFDEE/F/JJ
YETI/SNOW/MAN	YETI/SNOW/MAN
ORI/GIN/AL/212	ORI/GIN/AL/212
ADVERTISEMENT	ADVERITISEMENT
PERSONNEL/DEPT	PERSENNEL/DEPT
COM/PUT/ER/SYS/TEM	COM/PUT/ER/SyS/TEM
00/11/22/345/678	00/11/22/345/678
3456/0987/4321/32	3456/0987/4321/32
RO/AD/RU/NN/ER/234	RO/AD/RV/NN/ER/234
GAL/2001/200001/00	GAL/2001/20001/00
ISBN 0–561–15163–0	ISBN 0–561–15163–0
1010101/02020/300	1010101/02020/300
DATA-100/303/404/50	DATA/100/303/404/50

4. Coded instructions (2)

To enter the computer, type	LOG/SYS
To use the word processing package, type	WP
To use the database package, type	DB
To use the spreadsheets package, type	SPS
To open a new file, type	OF/NAME
To open and edit an old file, type	EF/NAME
To delete a file, type	DF/NAME

Example:

To enter the computer and edit an old database file
   Answer: LOG/SYS/DB/EF/NAME

Now try these (circle the correct answer):

Which code should be used for the following?

1   To enter the computer
   A. SYS/LOG
   B. EF/NAME/LOG/SYS
   C. LOG/SYS
   D. ON/COM/PU/TER
   E. None of these   *Answer*

2   To delete a file from the database (assume you have already entered the computer)
   A. DF/NAMEDB
   B. DB/DF/NAME
   C. DF/NAME/DB
   D. DF/NAME/SPS/WP/DB
   E. None of these   *Answer*

3   To enter the computer and create a new file on the word processor
   A. OF/NAME/WP
   B. OF/NAME/LOG/WP
   C. LOG/WP/NAME/OF
   D. LOG/SYS/WP/OF/NAME
   E. None of these   *Answer*

4   To edit a spreadsheet file by entering the computer first
   A. ED/SPS/LOG/SYS
   B. EF/NAME/SPS/LOG/SYS
   C. LOG/SYS/EF/SPS/NAME
   D. LOG/SYS/SPS/OF/NAME
   E. None of these   *Answer*

5   To delete a file from the word processing package

A. WP/EF/NAME/WP

B. DF/NAME/WP

C. WP/OF/NAME/

D. DF/LOG/NAME

E. None of these   *Answer* [ ]

6   To enter the computer and use the spreadsheets program

A. LOG/SYS/USE

B. LOG/SYS/SPS

C. USE/SPS/COM/PUT/ER

D. LOG/SPS/NAME

E. None of these   *Answer* [ ]

7   To use the database by logging on to the system

A. DB/LOG/SYS

B. LOG/DB/ON/TO/SYS

C. LOG/SYS/SPS

D. LOG/SYS/DB

E. None of these   *Answer* [ ]

8   To use the word processor to create a file once you have entered the computer

A. WP/NAME/LOG

B. LOG/WP/NAME

C. LOG/WP/OF

D. LOG/WP/NAME/OF

E. None of these   *Answer* [ ]

5. Coded instructions (3)

Checking databases

To enter the computer, type	LOG/SYS
To check database one, type	DBO
To check database two, type	DBT
To check database three, type	DBT/R
To delete a file from database, type	ND/followed by the code of the appropriate database
To create a file in the database, type	CF/followed by the database code

Which code should be used for the following?

1   To delete a file from database three (assume you have already entered the computer)

    A. DBT/R

    B. ND/LOG/DBT/R

    C. ND/DBT/R

    D. ND/DBO

    E. None of these   *Answer* [_____]

2   To check database two (assume you have already entered the computer)

    A. DBT

    B. DBO

    C. DBT/R

    D. DBO/T/R

    E. None of these   *Answer* [_____]

3   To enter the computer and check database one

  A. DBO

  B. LOG/SYS/DBO

  C. LOG/SYS/DBT/R

  D. DBT/R/O

  E. None of these   *Answer*

4   To create a file in database two (assume you have already entered the computer)

  A. LOG/SYS/CF/DBT

  B. CF/DBO/T

  C. CF/DBT

  D. ND/DBT

  E. None of these   *Answer*

5   To enter the computer and create a file in database three

  A. CF/DBT/R

  B. CF/DBT

  C. ND/DBT/R

  D. ND/DBT

  E. None of these   *Answer*

6   To enter the computer and delete a file in database one

  A. ND/DBO

  B. LOG/SYS/ND/DBO

  C. LOG/SYS/ND/DBT

  D. LOG/SYS/ND/DBT/R

  E. None of these   *Answer*

7 To enter the computer

A. LOG/SYS/DBO

B. LOG/SYS

C. LOG/ON/SYS

D. LOG/ON/DU/DE

E. None of these   *Answer* [   ]

8 To create a file in database two and then delete a file in database one (assume you have already entered the computer)

A. CF/DBO & CF/DBT

B. CF/DBT & CF/DBO

C. CF/DBT & ND/DBT

D. CF/DBT & ND/DBO

E. None of these   *Answer* [   ]

9 To enter the computer and check database three and then create a file in database two

A. LOG/SYS/DBT/R & CF/DBO

B. LOG/SYS/DBT/R & CF/DBT

C. LOG/SYS/DBT/R & CF/DBT/R

D. DBT/R & CF/DBT

E. None of these   *Answer* [   ]

10 To check database one, then create a file in database two and finally delete a file in database three (assume you have already logged on)

A. DBO & CF/DBT & ND/DBT/R

B. CF/DBO & DBO & ND/DBT/R

C. DBO & ND/DBT & CF/DBT/R

D. DBO/DBO/CF/DBT/RO/NG

E. None of these   *Answer* [   ]

6. Sequencing

In this exercise you have to put a list of events in a logical order. Under each list of events there are a number of boxes in which you are to put the numbers of the events in their logical order.

Example: Creating a file in a word processor

1. Load program   2. Switch on computer
3. Type   4. Switch off computer   5. Save file

Answer | 2 | 1 | 3 | 5 | 4 |

Now try these:

A   Going to work

1. Get on train   2. Get up   3. Go to platform

4. Get off train   5. Arrive at other end   6. Leave home

7. Get to station

Answer | | | | | | | |

B   Changing a wheel of a car

1. Put on spare wheel   2. Undo the bolts

3. Remove old wheel   4. Tighten bolts

Answer | | | | |

C   Using a cash dispenser machine

1. Input amount of money required

2. Type in correct number

3. Remove card and money

4. Insert card

Answer | | | | |

D Borrowing a book from a library

1. Take the book to the librarian
2. Locate the appropriate bookcase
3. Note the index code
4. Locate the appropriate section of the library
5. Consult the book location index
6. Locate the book

Answer ☐☐☐☐☐☐

E Solving a problem

1. Apply the solution   2. Identify the problem
3. Select the best solution
4. Suggest as many solutions as possible

Answer ☐☐☐☐

F Constructing a valid argument 1

1. Conclusion: Mary is a European
2. Germans are also Europeans
3. Mary is a German

Answer ☐☐☐

G Constructing a valid argument 2

1. Conclusion: Peter is not a European
2. Peter says he is an American subject
3. If he said he is American that means he cannot be European
4. Is Peter European?

Answer ☐☐☐☐

H   Tom is a tall person but he is not taller than Jeff. Tom is taller than both George and Ray. Jeff is shorter than Chris. Write the first letter of the tallest person's name.

Answer [ ]

I   Raheel is Naseem's son. Naseem has a brother called Khalid. The two brothers' father has a daughter, Gazala, who is older than Khalid but younger than Naseem. What is the relationship between Raheel and Gazala?

Answer [ ]

J   A car is being driven due north. After five miles it turns 180 degrees. Write the first letter of the direction in which the car is now travelling.

Answer [ ]

In the Kogan Page testing series you will find thousands more practice questions at the intermediate level. We recommend:

The Numeracy Test Workbook – contains over 700 practice questions
The Verbal Reasoning Test Workbook – contains over 700 practice questions
Ultimate Psychometric Tests – contains over 1,000 practice questions

At the advanced level we recommend:

How to pass Graduate Psychometric Tests, 3rd edition
How to pass Advanced Numeracy Tests, revised edition
How to pass Advanced Verbal Reasoning Tests

CHAPTER 6

Answers and explanations

Chapter 4. Some of the most common types of test

1. Verbal tests that measure comprehension (page 25)

A. Swapping words

First example   'test' and 'hard'
Second example   'limit' and 'virtually'

B. Finding missing words

B

C. Locating words that mean the same or the opposite

First example   C
Second example B

2. Tests of grammar and punctuation (page 26)

A. Choosing from a number of sentences

First example   C
Second example   A

B. Choosing from pairs of words

First example   D
Second example   D

3. Spelling tests (page 28)

Example 1
You should have underlined:
sincerely, foreign, immediate, merchandise, shampoo

Example 2
You should have written out the following words:
balance, beautify, correlate, disease

Example 3
Question 1   1, 18, 20
Question 2   21, 5, 19

4. Tests of logical thinking (page 30)

A. Following instructions

Example 1   B
Example 2   C

B. Relationships between numbers and statements

Example 1   15. Each number is 4 greater than the previous one.
Example 2   D. Stoke on Trent (all the others are islands)
Example 3   16. All the others can be divided by 5.
Example 4   C. All the others have two lines in the box.

5. Numerical tests (page 32)

A. Numerical reasoning

Example 1	£15
Example 2	£73.52
Example 3	£25
Example 4	£21

B. Estimating/approximating

Example 1	D
Example 2	A

C. Percentages and other fractions

Example 1	$1\frac{5}{12}$
Example 2	A
Example 3	£6.75
Example 4	£752
Example 5	£91.20
Example 6	B

6. Tests of clerical and computing skills (page 34)

A. Flow diagrams

2

B. Sequencing

4, 5, 2, 3, 1

C. Coded instructions

1	OF
2	DFESC
3	OFSPSF

D. Checking computer data

#	Company		Address		Town		Postcode	
1	Land Scales Ltd	N	9 Lanca Place	N	Lancaster	Y	ES2 5HJ	Y
2	Fox Associates	Y	143 West Side	Y	Ealing	Y	5HJ 6TT	Y
3	Collers Building	N	68 Cambridge Street	Y	Queeens Way	N	3DD 5TG	Y
4	Top Creation	Y	11 Gorge Road	N	Plaistow	Y	9NN 4RF	Y
5	Victoria Pack Systems	N	34a Major Street	Y	Great Harwood	Y	2DE 6VC	Y
6	Municipal Supplies	Y	22 Warehouse Road	Y	Small Health	N	8MN 6AS	Y
7	Barton Hotel	N	78 Baker Street	Y	Uxbrige	N	12DD 5TT	N
8	Save Finances	N	53 Church Yard Close	Y	Sherman	Y	7FC 4DX	Y
9	Longsdale LTD	N	2 Burton Street	Y	Hackney	Y	E5 2CD	Y
10	Western Electronic	N	10 Resister Road	N	EastHam	N	E9 4RF	N
11	New Technology	N	13 Forth Avenue	N	Manor Park	Y	E12 5NT	Y
12	Net Surfing Cafe	Y	20 Cyber Street	Y	Compton	Y	CB13 7FG	Y
13	Super Robotics PLC	N	145 Well Street	N	High Grove	N	HG8 2WL	Y
14	Info Tech Ltd	Y	1 New Lane	Y	Hertfordshire	Y	NW3 25A	N
15	Printers Printers	N	2 Print Street	N	Printington	Y	PTS 2PR	N

Chapter 5. Practice material

Verbal tests (pages 45–47)

1. The same meaning or the opposite (page 45)

	Opposites	Same
store	waste	stockpile
wrong	right	mistaken
question	answer	enquire
measure	guesswork	gauge
problem	solution	obstacle
obscure	transparent	conceal
synthetic	natural	man-made
vertical	horizontal	upright
repair	neglect	recondition
strengthen	weaken	augment

1 pedalo
2 ability
3 brawl
4 mud
5 short

2. Sound alike/look alike words (page 47)

Exercise 1

1 bore, boar
2 specific, Pacific
3 morning, mourning
4 principle, principal
5 waist, waste
6 there, their

Exercise 2

1 knew   4 rap
2 too   5 few
3 guerrillas   6 draft

7	quiet	**17**	off
8	rites	**18**	patients
9	alms	**19**	through
10	lead	**20**	seat
11	affecting	**21**	heard
12	whether	**22**	hoarse
13	accepted	**23**	mail
14	feat	**24**	scene
15	there	**25**	except
16	cite	**26**	their

3. Choosing the right word (page 51)

1	there	**5**	nor
2	eaten	**6**	that
3	has	**7**	were
4	as though	**8**	I

4. Timed exercise – choosing the right word (page 53)

1	knew	leaving
2	you	have
3	able	woman
4	weather	fine
5	flew	across
6	agree	differ
7	tired	colour
8	column	rows
9	program	used
10	centre	manager

5. Choosing the right sentence (page 55)

1	B
2	A
3	A
4	A
5	C

6. Timed exercise – choosing the right sentence (page 57)

1	C	**6**	D
2	B	**7**	D
3	B	**8**	C
4	C	**9**	E
5	A	**10**	D

7. Plural words (page 59)

1	C	**19**	B
2	D	**20**	D
3	B	**21**	C
4	B	**22**	B
5	B	**23**	A
6	E	**24**	A
7	D	**25**	B
8	A	**26**	B
9	E	**27**	B
10	D	**28**	A
11	D	**29**	B
12	D	**30**	A
13	A	**31**	E
14	B	**32**	B
15	A	**33**	C
16	B	**34**	B
17	C	**35**	E
18	A		

8. Spelling (page 66)

1	67	17	20	48
2	27	7		
3	41	34		
4	12	21	46	
5	15	20		
6	28	56	73	55
7	5	19	30	74
8	67	22	65	24

9. Timed spelling (page 70)

1	8	46	47	
2	38	72	7	58
3	14	32	11	71
4	18	24		
5	75	41	43	
6	5	13	65	29
7	55	12	6	56
8	57	62	59	
9	48	64	39	73
10	54	74	67	

10. Reading for information (page 73)

1   False
2   False
3   True
4   True
5   False
6   False
7   False
8   False
9   True

A different style of reading for information question

1   *Answer*: Cannot tell
Explanation: The passage does not say which of the inner planets is closest to the sun.

2   *Answer*: True
Explanation: The passage states that all the outer planets have moons.

3   *Answer*: False
Explanation: The passage states that there are five, the four large gaseous planets and Pluto.

4 *Answer*: False
Explanation: Mars is described as one of the inner planets while Jupiter is described as one of the outer planets. From this it can be inferred that Jupiter is further from the sun than Mars.

5 *Answer*: True
Explanation: The passage states that the number of sufferers from high blood pressure is forecast to rise further both in developed and developing countries.

6 *Answer*: Cannot tell
Explanation: The passage states that it is estimated that 1 billion people suffer from high blood pressure but the passage does not indicate how many will die as a result of suffering this condition.

7 *Answer*: False
Explanation: The passage states ways in which it can be reduced.

8 *Answer*: Cannot tell
Explanation: The passage does not provide information on this point.

9 *Answer*: False
Explanation: The passage states that the moon provides twice the gravitation pull of the sun but this still means that the sun's gravitational force contributes to the tidal effect.

10 *Answer*: Cannot tell
Explanation: The locations of the occurrences are not detailed in the passages.

11 *Answer*: Cannot tell
Explanation: The passage makes no comment on this issue.

12 *Answer*: True
        Explanation: The passage states that the second bulge is caused this way.

13 *Answer*: True
        Explanation: The passage states that the medieval period lasted from 1000 to 1500, which is 500 years.

14 *Answer*: True
        Explanation: The passage states that most people lived in the countryside.

15 *Answer*: Cannot tell
        Explanation: The passage does not provide any information on the effect of a bad harvest.

16 *Answer*: False
        Explanation: The passage states that the Dark Ages preceded the medieval period, which means the Dark Ages were before the medieval period.

17 *Answer*: False
        Explanation: The passage states that the heating effect might cause harm to our brains but it does not say that it could warm brain tissue.

18 *Answer*: True
        Explanation: The passage states that mobile phones work by transmitting and receiving radio waves and that these waves create electromagnetic fields.

19 *Answer*: True
        Explanation: The passage states that they are a part of the spectrum along with visible light, microwaves and x-rays.

20 *Answer*: Cannot tell
        Explanation: The passage provides no information on the susceptibility of children.

21   *Answer*: Cannot tell
Explanation: The passage provides no information on the accuracy of forecasts made from these test scores.

22   *Answer*: False
Explanation: The passage does not state this.

23   *Answer*: True
Explanation: As adults they had gone on to realise average scores.

24   *Answer*: Cannot tell
Explanation: The passage provides no explanation for the differences in the groups' performances.

25   *Answer*: True
Explanation: Immigration and emigration affect the population of particular areas but not the world population as a whole.

26   *Answer*: False
Explanation: The passage states that the population is determined by the balance between birth and death rates and a higher birth rate may not result in a higher world population if the death rate also increases.

27   *Answer*: Cannot tell
Explanation: The passage provides no information on the future expected growth or decline of the world's population.

28   *Answer*: False
Explanation: Higher immigration into an area will lead the population to increase not decrease.

29   *Answer*: False
Explanation: The passage does not state anything about the languages spoken by Americans.

30   *Answer*: False
Explanation: The passage states that America's wealth is also derived from other factors.

31   *Answer*: Cannot tell
Explanation: While we all know this is true it is not stated in the passage so you must conclude that we cannot tell.

32   *Answer*: True
Explanation: America is the third most populous nation with 281 million people so the next most populous must have a population smaller than this.

33   *Answer*: True
Explanation: The passage states that to the south of the Azores lie Madeira and the Canaries.

34   *Answer*: Cannot tell
Explanation: The passage does not say whether or not the Azores are a developed holiday destination.

35   *Answer*: False
Explanation: St Helena is described as further south of the Cape Verde Islands.

36   *Answer*: True
Explanation: The passage states that the Cape Verde Islands and all islands south are much quieter.

37   *Answer*: Cannot tell
Explanation: The passage does not indicate what might be proportionate fines for particular offences.

38   *Answer*: False
Explanation: They prefer a system where the level of fine is proportionate to the seriousness of the crime.

39 *Answer*: True

Explanation: Provided that they were in the same income bracket.

40 *Answer*: False

Explanation: The passage states that commentators concluded that the public prefer a system where a fine acts as a deterrent and for this to happen the person fined should to some extent struggle to pay it. For this to happen the fine must still bear some relationship to the offender's income.

11. Alphabetical order (page 87)

Arranging words – Example 1

1	Acrobat	**5**	Orator
2	Gangster	**6**	Puff adder
3	Heiress	**7**	Reptile
4	Kidnap	**8**	Sorrow

Arranging words – Example 2

1	Fabric	**5**	February
2	Faithful	**6**	Fixer
3	Farmyard	**7**	Florida
4	Feather	**8**	Foliage

Rearranging letters

1	achirty	**5**	hip
2	iloqru	**6**	deny
3	acginor	**7**	lot
4	aehmst	**8**	bmr

Timed exercise

Name	*File Number*	*Name*	*File Number*
Young	18	Warner	18
Bayard	3	Carrington	5
Harvey	9	Christie	5
Fisher	8	Tooling	16

Skinner	15		Arnold	2
Bishop	3		Hood	9
Adler	1		Dell	7

12. Comparisons 1 (page 90)

1	B	2	C	3	A	4	C	5	C
6	B	7	B	8	B	9	B	10	B
11	B	12	C	13	C	14	B	15	D

13. Comparisons 2 (page 92)

1	B	2	C	3	A	4	C	5	A
6	B	7	C	8	A	9	C	10	B
11	B	12	B	13	B	14	B	15	C

14. Odd-one-out (page 94)

| 1 | A | 2 | D | 3 | D | 4 | E | 5 | E | 6 | C |
| 7 | E | 8 | D | 9 | C | 10 | C | 11 | A | 12 | E |

15. Opposites (page 96)

| 1 | B | 2 | B | 3 | C | 4 | B | 5 | C |
| 6 | B | 7 | A | 8 | B | 9 | B | 10 | C |

16. Similar sounding words (page 97)

Exercise 1

1	cite/site	2	coarse	3	draught
4	brooch	5	knew	6	damn
7	whether	8	dew	9	male
10	dye	11	Gail/Gayle	12	suite
13	right/wright/rite	14	too/two	15	reed
16	tale	17	buy/by	18	won
19	waive	20	four/fore	21	knead
22	flour	23	breech	24	soul
25	scene	26	hare	27	son
28	herd	29	seam	30	hart

Exercise 2

1	fete	**2**	here	**3**	grate
4	whole	**5**	know	**6**	mane
7	board	**8**	ail	**9**	bald
10	knight	**11**	bear	**12**	nit
13	break	**14**	minor	**15**	bred
16	navel	**17**	scent	**18**	nun
19	meat	**20**	oar/ore	**21**	off
22	piece	**23**	peal	**24**	pear
25	peak	**26**	plait	**27**	poll
28	pool	**29**	pore	**30**	reign/rein
31	prey	**32**	programme	**33**	purl
34	quay	**35**	wrest	**36**	wrap
37	wreak	**38**	wring	**39**	wry
40	shoo				

18. Homophones (page 99)

1	hymn	**2**	site/cite	**3**	bald	**4**	seam
5	bean	**6**	wring	**7**	write/wright	**8**	knight
9	fort	**10**	through	**11**	bough	**12**	wrung
13	pane	**14**	weight	**15**	break	**16**	grate
17	knew	**18**	know	**19**	sea	**20**	wear

19. More homophones (page 99)

1	hear	**2**	bear	**3**	fare	**4**	hare
5	tee	**6**	pair	**7**	deer	**8**	four/fore
9	bait	**10**	fete	**11**	bail	**12**	sail
13	ail	**14**	tail	**15**	veil	**16**	wail
17	witch	**18**	pail	**19**	wore	**20**	son

20. Homophones again (page 100)

1	mail	**2**	to/too	**3**	so	**4**	whole
5	flair	**6**	doe	**7**	quay	**8**	plane
9	cheque	**10**	fir	**11**	knot	**12**	cue
13	leek	**14**	feat	**15**	beet	**16**	boar
17	board	**18**	ewe	**19**	suite	**20**	tyre

21. Synonyms (page 101)

1	Nearby	**Close**		11	Brawl	**Fight**
2	Climb	**Ascend**		12	Foe	**Enemy**
3	Absolute	**Complete**		13	Idea	**Concept**
4	Foreign	**Alien**		14	Kidnap	**Abduct**
5	Abuse	**Misuse**		15	Alike	**Similar**
6	Distant	**Far**		16	Behind	**Rear**
7	Ocean	**Sea**		17	Benefit	**Advantage**
8	Arbiter	**Judge**		18	Garbage	**Rubbish**
9	Mate	**Friend**		19	Outlaw	**Bandit**
10	Aroma	**Fragrance**		20	Sound	**Audio**

22. More synonyms (page 102)

1	Empty	**Blank**		11	Border	**Boundary**
2	Wound	**Gash**		12	Pester	**Bother**
3	Least	**Smallest**		13	Fragile	**Brittle**
4	Grab	**Seize**		14	Inferior	**Crummy**
5	Channel	**Groove**		15	Lavatory	**Latrine**
6	Insect	**Bug**		16	Oppose	**Counter**
7	Refuse	**Garbage**		17	Sneer	**Fleer**
8	Jail	**Gaol**		18	Shut	**Close**
9	Sham	**Bogus**		19	Gift	**Present**
10	Drum	**Bongo**		20	Cheese	**Curd**

1	Rude	**Insolent**		11	Insane	**Mad**
2	Sailor	**Mariner**		12	Smell	**Odour**
3	Foe	**Enemy**		13	Dampness	**Moisture**
4	Unite	**Join**		14	Forbid	**Prohibit**
5	Fable	**Myth**		15	Wide	**Broad**
6	Sharp	**Acute**		16	Control	**Curb**
7	Weariness	**Fatigue**		17	Rough	**Coarse**
8	Feeble	**Weak**		18	Hide	**Conceal**
9	Round	**Circular**		19	Inside	**Interior**
10	Dwelling	**Abode**		20	Hard	**Difficult**

1	Peaceful	**Tranquil**		11	Anger	**Wrath**
2	Clear	**Transparent**		12	Quick	**Rapid**
3	Riches	**Wealth**		13	Purchase	**Buy**
4	Strict	**Stern**		14	Pointless	**Futile**
5	Horse	**Steed**		15	Cure	**Remedy**
6	Slim	**Slender**		16	Show	**Reveal**
7	Position	**Rank**		17	Strong	**Sturdy**
8	Empty	**Vacant**		18	Yield	**Surrender**
9	Annually	**Yearly**		19	Smooth	**Sleek**
10	Defeat	**Vanquish**		20	Hang	**Suspend**

23. Antonyms (page 104)

1	Flexible	Rigid (6)
2	Solid	Liquid (9)
3	Shiny	Dull (4)
4	Enemy	Friend (19)
5	High	Low (8)
6	Above	Below (16)
7	Back	Front (12)
8	Left	Right (14)
9	Shut	Open (17)
10	Bad	Good (10)

24. More antonyms (page 106)

1	Empty	Full (6)
2	Last	First (17)
3	Fluid	Solid (4)
4	Increment	Decrease (12)
5	Loose	Fixed (8)
6	Motivate	Discourage (11)
7	Extract	Replace (7)
8	Plural	Singular (13)
9	Pliable	Rigid (16)
10	Plenty	Scarce (19)

25. Creating compound words (page 106)

1	Sun	Day	**2**	He	Art
3	Motor	Car	**4**	Flip	Side
5	After	Noon	**6**	Allow	Able
7	Alpha	Bet	**8**	Amalgam	Ate
9	Anti	Body	**10**	Anti	Christ
11	Anti	Social	**12**	Audio	Meter
13	Auto	Graph	**14**	Auto	Mate
15	Back	Hand	**16**	Back	Ache
17	Back	Ward	**18**	Bag	Pipe
19	High	Land	**20**	Rail	Way
21	Base	Ball	**22**	Bat	Ten
23	Be	Come	**24**	Bed	Clothes
25	Bed	Pan			

26. More compound words (page 108)

1	Blind	Date	**2**	Block	Age
3	Bother	Some	**4**	Top	Less
5	Blind	Spot	**6**	Bread	Crumb
7	Break	Fast	**8**	Blind	Fold
9	Bride	Groom	**10**	Brief	Case
11	Brute	Force	**12**	Break	Able
13	Chain	Saw	**14**	Chair	Man
15	Chamber	Maid	**16**	Brides	Maid

17	Colour	Blind	18	Common	Wealth
19	Copy	Right	20	Corn	Wall
21	Counter	Foil	22	Crash	Land
23	Counter	Balance	24	Counter	Act
25	Table	Spoon			

27. Compound words again (page 109)

1	Coat	Hanger	2	Gear	Stick
3	Import	Ant	4	Home	Work
5	Honey	Comb	6	Hour	Glass
7	Man	Kind	8	Dead	Line
9	Ice	Cream	10	Honey	Moon
11	Honey	Pot	12	Bed	Linen
13	Beet	Root	14	Be	Hold
15	Birth	Day	16	Black	Head
17	Church	Warden	18	Class	Less
19	Cloak	Room	20	Grand	Father
21	Coast	Guard	22	Fat	Her
23	Game	Keeper	24	Plat	Form
25	Sat	Urn			

28. Four-minute compound words (page 110)

1	Broad	Cast	2	Brother	Hood
3	Bump	Kin	4	Bus	King
5	Cap	Able	6	Care	Less
7	Car	Rot	8	Check	Mate
9	Car	Ton	10	Broad	Way
11	Common	Place	12	Complain	Ant
13	Gentle	Man	14	Gate	Way
15	For	Given	16	Fox	Hound
17	Fond	Ant	18	Foot	Steps
19	Eye	Brow	20	Feat	Her
21	Fabric	Ate	22	Friend	Ship
23	Foot	Path	24	Game	Keeper
25	Cool	Ant			

29. Three-minute compound words (page 111)

1	Fruit	Less	**2**	Gain	Fully
3	For	Ward	**4**	Four	Some
5	Frame	Work	**6**	Land	Mark
7	Eye	Lid	**8**	Fare	Well
9	Cot	Ton	**10**	Feed	Back
11	For	Tune	**12**	Gate	Crash
13	Fly	Wheel	**14**	God	Son
15	For	Age	**16**	Flash	Back
17	Dart	Mouth	**18**	Eye	Sight
19	Under	Mine	**20**	Count	Less
21	Good	Will	**22**	Grand	Stand
23	Fly	Over	**24**	Counter	Part
25	Foot	Hold			

30. Analogies (page 112)

1	B fly	**2**	C pup	**3**	D couple
4	B fish	**5**	A daughter	**6**	B December
7	C orange	**8**	C wires	**9**	D flock
10	A east	**11**	B commence	**12**	A foot
13	B peruse	**14**	A museum	**15**	A automobile
16	D pride	**17**	B plague	**18**	C troop
19	A school	**20**	B troupe	**21**	C library
22	B leap	**23**	C mass	**24**	B two
25	C elver				

Numerical tests (pages 115–140)

1. Approximating (pages 116–133)

Rounding off numbers (1)

1	100	**2**	10	**3**	2
4	9	**5**	8	**6**	500
7	115	**8**	6	**9**	3
10	6	**11**	2	**12**	8
13	6	**14**	8	**15**	45

Rounding off numbers (2)

1	20% of 700	**9**	50% of 800
2	100% of 50	**10**	40% of 80
3	50% of 60	**11**	10% of 40
4	20% of 1000	**12**	5% of 50
5	50% of 200	**13**	5% of 100
6	20% of 100	**14**	120% of 1000
7	200% of 100	**15**	10% of 700
8	10% of 900		

Rounding off numbers (3)

1	15	**9**	1
2	552	**10**	2
3	8	**11**	17
4	300	**12**	800
5	200	**13**	600
6	14000	**14**	5
7	3500	**15**	5
8	2000		

Addition

1	448.49	**6**	150
2	6232	**7**	506
3	998	**8**	1230
4	7197.6	**9**	15100
5	100.916	**10**	7430

Subtraction

1	122	**6**	463
2	27	**7**	4795
3	1.92	**8**	229
4	2488	**9**	9587.88
5	10.22	**10**	73.85

Multiplication

1	1475	**6**	165
2	14820	**7**	10000
3	125	**8**	30000
4	1650	**9**	99.99
5	2500	**10**	49.95

Division

1	8.2	**4**	110
2	22	**5**	990
3	1.8		

Percentages

1	50	**6**	201.55
2	120	**7**	17.28
3	329.67	**8**	72
4	367.01	**9**	2090
5	250	**10**	450

Fractions

1	13¾	**4**	31
2	8	**5**	2¹/₁₂
3	60		

Mixed

1	99	**2**	80	**3**	9.31
4	162	**5**	43.88	**6**	75.4
7	142.45	**8**	70.41	**9**	1233
10	1111	**11**	5472	**12**	5

More percentages and some essential ratios

1 *Answer*: 50%
    Explanation: $100 \div 2 = 50 \times 1 = 50$

2 *Answer*: 25%
    Explanation: $100 \div 4 = 25 \times 1 = 25$

3 *Answer*: 33.3%
   Explanation: $100 \div 3 = 33.3 \times 1 = 33.3$

4 *Answer*: 20%
   Explanation: $100 \div 5 = 20 \times 1 = 20$

5 *Answer*: 12.5%
   Explanation: $100 \div 8 = 12.5 \times 1 = 12.5$

6 *Answer*: 6.25%
   Explanation: $100 \div 16 = 6.25 \times 1 = 6.25$

7 *Answer*: 8.3%
   Explanation: $100 \div 12 = 8.3 \times 1 = 8.3$

8 *Answer*: 11.1%
   Explanation: $100 \div 9 = 11.1 \times 1 = 11.1$

9 *Answer*: 66.6%
   Explanation: $100 \div 3 = 33.3 \times 2 = 66.6$

10 *Answer*: 60%
   Explanation: $100 \div 5 = 20 \times 3 = 60$

11 *Answer*: 37.5%
   Explanation: $100 \div 16 = 6.25 \times 6 = 37.5$

12 *Answer*: 62.5%
   Explanation: $100 \div 8 = 12.5 \times 5 = 62.5$

Changing between decimals and percentages

1 *Answer*: 50%
   Explanation: $0.5 \times 100 = 50$

2 *Answer*: 20%
   Explanation: $0.2 \times 100 = 20$

3   *Answer*: 60%
      Explanation: $0.6 \times 100 = 60$

4   *Answer*: 40%
      Explanation: $0.4 \times 100 = 40$

5   *Answer*: 35%
      Explanation: $0.35 \times 100 = 35$

6   *Answer*: 72%
      Explanation: $0.72 \times 100 = 72$

7   *Answer*: 42.5%
      Explanation: $0.425 \times 100 = 42.5$

8   *Answer*: 33.3%
      Explanation: $0.333 \times 100 = 33.3$

9   *Answer*: 53.25%
      Explanation: $0.5325 \times 100 = 53.25$

10   *Answer*: 0.25
      Explanation: $25 \div 100 = 0.25$

11   *Answer*: 0.9
      Explanation: $90 \div 100 = 0.9$

12   *Answer*: 0.05
      Explanation: $5 \div 100 = 0.05$

13   *Answer*: 0.15
      Explanation: $15 \div 100 = 0.15$

14   *Answer*: 0.024
      Explanation: $2.4 \div 100 = 0.024$

15 *Answer*: 0.006
   Explanation: $0.6 \div 100 = 0.006$

A value expressed as a percentage of another

1 *Answer*: 30%
   Explanation: $15 \div 50 = 0.3 \times 100 = 30$

2 *Answer*: 12%
   Explanation: $3 \div 25 = 0.12 \times 100 = 12$

3 *Answer*: 12.5%
   Explanation: $5 \div 40 = 0.125 \times 100 = 12.5$

4 *Answer*: 20%
   Explanation: $1 \div 5 = 0.2 \times 100 = 20$

5 *Answer*: 8%
   Explanation: $6 \div 75 = 0.08 \times 100 = 8$

6 *Answer*: 80%
   Explanation: $10 \div 12.5 = 0.8 \times 100 = 80$

7 *Answer*: 12.5%
   Explanation: $2 \div 16 = 0.125 \times 100 = 12.5$

8 *Answer*: 5%
   Explanation: $4 \div 80 = 0.05 \times 100 = 5$

9 *Answer*: 30%
   Explanation: $12 \div 40 = 0.3 \times 100 = 30$

10 *Answer*: 40%
   Explanation: $28 \div 70 = 0.4 \times 100 = 40$

Finding percentages of quantities

1 *Answer*: £32
   Explanation: $0.4 \times 80 = 32$

2 *Answer*: 45 minutes
   Explanation: Convert the hours into minutes, $3 \times 60 = 180$,
   $0.25 \times 180 = 45$

3 *Answer*: 6 metres
   Explanation: $0.15 \times 40 = 6$

4 *Answer*: £1.80
   Explanation: $0.2 \times 9 = 1.8$

5 *Answer*: 600cm
   Explanation: $0.05 \times 12 = 0.6$

6 *Answer*: 1 hour and 12 minutes
   Explanation: 720 minutes $\times 0.1 = 72 = 1$ hour and 12 minutes

7 *Answer*: £78
   Explanation: $0.15 \times 520 = 78$

8 *Answer*: 27 minutes
   Explanation: 90 minutes $\times 0.3 = 27$

9 *Answer*: 3m, 660cm
   Explanation: $0.2 \times 18.3 = 3.66$

10 *Answer*: 52 minutes and 30 seconds
   Explanation: $5 \times 60 = 300$ minutes, $300 \times 0.175 = 52.5 = 52$
   minutes and 30 seconds

Percentage increase

1   *Answer*: 50%
   Explanation: 10 (the increase) $\div$ 20 = 0.5 $\times$ 100 = 50

2   *Answer*: 20%
   Explanation: 8 $\div$ 40 = 0.2 $\times$ 100 = 20

3   *Answer*: 33.3%
   Explanation: 6 $\div$ 18 = 0.33 $\times$ 100 = 33.3

4   *Answer*: 40%
   Explanation: 32 $\div$ 80 = 0.4 $\times$ 100 = 40

5   *Answer*: 60%
   Explanation: 6.6 $\div$ 11 = 0.6 $\times$ 100 = 60

6   *Answer*: 30%
   Explanation: 7.5 $\div$ 25 = 0.3 $\times$ 100 = 30

7   *Answer*: 8%
   Explanation: 7.2 $\div$ 90 = 0.08 $\times$ 100 = 8

8   *Answer*: 12.5%
   Explanation: 1 $\div$ 8 = 0.125 $\times$ 100 = 12.5

9   *Answer*: 4%
   Explanation: 4.8 $\div$ 120 = 0.04 $\times$ 100 = 4

10   *Answer*: 60%
   Explanation: 21.6 $\div$ 36 = 0.6 $\times$ 100 = 60

Percentage decrease

1   *Answer*: 5%
   Explanation: 5 $\div$ 100 = 0.05 $\times$ 100 = 5

2   *Answer*: 16%
    Explanation: $8 \div 50 = 0.16 \times 100 = 16$

3   *Answer*: 24%
    Explanation: $18 \div 75 = 0.24 \times 100 = 24$

4   *Answer*: 45%
    Explanation: $36 \div 80 = 0.45 \times 100 = 45$

5   *Answer*: 60%
    Explanation: $72 \div 120 = 0.6 \times 100 = 60$

6   *Answer*: 75%
    Explanation: $6 \div 8 = 0.75 \times 100 = 75$

7   *Answer*: 90%
    Explanation: $81 \div 90 = 0.9 \times 100 = 90$

8   *Answer*: 30%
    Explanation: $7.5 \div 25 = 0.3 \times 100 = 30$

9   *Answer*: 12%
    Explanation: $3.6 \div 30 = 0.12 \times 100 = 12$

10 *Answer*: 22%
    Explanation: $14.3 \div 65 = 0.22 \times 100 = 22$

Percentage profit or loss

1   *Answer*: 20% profit
    Explanation: $2 \div 10 = 0.2 \times 100 = 20$

2   *Answer*: 20% loss
    Explanation: $8 \div 40 = 0.2 \times 100 = 20$

3   *Answer*: 40% profit
    Explanation: $20 \div 50 = 0.4 \times 100 = 40$

4   *Answer*: 12.5% loss
   Explanation: $1 \div 8 = 0.125 \times 100 = 12.5$

5   *Answer*: 30% profit
   Explanation: $7.5 \div 25 = 0.3 \times 100 = 30$

6   *Answer*: 80% loss
   Explanation: $9.6 \div 12 = 0.8 \times 100 = 80$

7   *Answer*: 15% profit
   Explanation: $0.75 \div 5 = 0.15 \times 100 = 15$

8   *Answer*: 70% loss
   Explanation: $31.5 \div 45 = 0.7 \times 100 = 70$

9   *Answer*: 60% profit
   Explanation: $42 \div 70 = 0.6 \times 100 = 60$

10   *Answer*: 6% loss
   Explanation: $0.39 \div 6.5 = 0.06 \times 100 = 6$

Ratios

1   *Answer*: 80 : 20
   Explanation: $4 + 1 = 5$, $100 \div 5 = 20$, $4 \times 20 = 80$, $1 \times 20 = 20$

2   *Answer*: 21 : 28
   Explanation: $3 + 4 = 7$, $49 \div 7 = 7$, $3 \times 7 = 21$, $4 \times 7 = 28$

3   *Answer*: 6 : 30
   Explanation: $1 + 5 = 6$, $36 \div 6 = 6$, $1 \times 6 = 6$, $5 \times 6 = 30$

4   *Answer*: 45 : 27
   Explanation: $5 + 3 = 8$, $72 \div 8 = 9$, $5 \times 9 = 45$, $3 \times 9 = 27$

5   *Answer*: 33 : 22
   Explanation: $3 + 2 = 5$, $55 \div 5 = 11$, $3 \times 11 = 33$, $2 \times 11 = 22$

6 *Answer*: 13 : 91 : 26
Explanation: 1 + 7 + 2 = 10, 130 ÷ 10 = 13, 1 × 13 = 13, 7 × 13 = 91, 2 × 13 = 26

7 *Answer*: 24 : 16 : 12
Explanation: 6 + 4 + 3 = 13, 52 ÷ 13 = 4, 6 × 4 = 24, 4 × 4 = 16, 3 × 4 = 12

8 *Answer*: 17.5 : 7.5 : 30
Explanation: 7 + 3 + 12 = 22, 55 ÷ 22 = 2.5, 7 × 2.5 = 17.5, 3 × 2.5 = 7.5, 12 × 2.5 = 30

9 *Answer*: 3.5 : 14 : 10.5
Explanation: 1 + 4 + 3 = 8, 28 ÷ 8 = 3.5, 1 × 3.5 = 3.5, 4 × 3.5 = 14, 3 × 3.5 = 10.5

10 *Answer*: 11 : 27.5 : 22
Explanation: 2 + 5 + 4 = 11, 60.5 ÷ 11 = 5.5, 2 × 5.5 = 11, 5 × 5.5 = 27.5, 4 × 5.5 = 22

2. Numerical reasoning (pages 133–140)

1 £12.00
2 £55.66
3 22½ hours
4 5,250 people
5 £176.25
6 £572
7 £9,750
8 £12,000
9 £13
10 (a) £1,665
(b) £555
11 £37.50
12 £37.50
13 £25
14 £300.88

Timed practical numerical problems

1   £10.70

2   £15.40

3   85.6 pence

4   25%
    Explanation: 8 + 5 = 13 so find 13 as a percentage of 52
    (the number of weeks in a year). 52 = 100%, 1% = 0.52
    (52 ÷ 100), 13 ÷ 0.52 = 25 or 25%

5   63
    Explanation: ¼ of 180 = 45 (180 ÷ 4) houses for workers in
    essential services, 2/5 of 180 = 72 (180 ÷ 5 × 2) homes for
    homeless families which leaves 63 (180 − 45 = 135 − 72)
    to be sold.

6   45%
    Explanation: 5 = 100%, 1% = 0.05. The increase = 2.25 days,
    2.25 ÷ 0.05 = 45%.

7   Neither − they represent the same value
    Explanation: find the price of each per gram to compare.
    $3.60 ÷ 300 = $0.012 per gram, $12 ÷ 1,000 = 0.012 also.

8   6
    Explanation: 12 in 60 = 1 in 5 successful bids = a 20%
    success rate, 20 × ¾ = 15. So the new success rate = 15%
    and 15% of 40 = 6.

9 $30.40
    Explanation: 16 ÷ 50 = 0.32 per pencil × 70 = $22.40,
    48 ÷ 6 = $8 a tray. 132 ÷ 6 = 22 eggs on each tray,
    so 22 eggs = $8 + $22.40 = $30.4

10   190,000
    Explanation: 203,775 = 104.5%, 100% = 203,
    775 ÷ 104.5 = 195,000

Foreign currency exchange rates

1   D (130)
2   E (None of these)
3   C (12.60)
4   C (300)
5   B (6,500)
6   D (110)
7   D (1,250, 375, 625,000)
8   B (337.78)
9   C (4,722.22)
10 B (3,600)

Clerical tests (pages 140–177)

1. Coded instructions (page 140)

Exercise 1
1   Down the launderette
2   Watching the news on TV
3   12.00
4   Paying the milk bill
5   12.00
6   9 am

Exercise 2

1	udyne	lippgai	nitco	modod
2	Tratma	nitco	udyne	lippgai
3	ranch	udyne	modod	lippgai

Into English
4   Fido the dog
5   Is Fido black?
6   Is the dog Fido?

Exercise 3
1   D   2   B   3   D

Timed coded instructions exercise

1	D	**4**	D
2	D	**5**	D
3	B		

Exercise 4

1 15 years

2 1hr and 3 min
(63 min)

3 3.6 kg
(3600 grams)

4 7 years

5 17,280 packets

6 £1.50

7 5.64m

8 73.10kg

9 Raheel = 1.99m
and Adeel = 1.75m

10 Total £67,200
Average £16,800

11 3,600 words

12 400 women

13 £450

14 £600

15 36 sweets

Exercise 5

1	7	**2**	2	**3**	16	**4**	0	**5**	10
6	4	**7**	6	**8**	26	**9**	6	**10**	10

Exercise 6

1	110	**2**	96	**3**	5	**4**	26

Exercise 7

1	J	**2**	G	**3**	P	**4**	X	**5**	B
6	G	**7**	J	**8**	J	**9**	S	**10**	Y
11	T	**12**	F	**13**	U	**14**	V	**15**	C
16	150	**17**	156	**18**	28	**19**	75	**20**	27

Exercise 8

1	D	**2**	A	**3**	D	**4**	B	**5**	E
6	E	**7**	C	**8**	D	**9**	D	**10**	A

Exercise 9

1

35
63 ÷ 9
5

2

18
12 × 3
2

3

72
62 − 26
36

4

11
61 − 59
9

5

−7
−22 + 36
21

6

8
4 × 16
8

7

42
21 + 56
35

8

121
22 ÷ 2
11

9

0
12 × 0
99

10

6
16 × 3
8

11

−10
−5 × 4
2

12

93
153 − 111
51

Exercise 10

1

11
15 $+$ 34
38

2

12
9 $\times$ 24
18

3

216
180 $\div$ 15
18

4

216
326 $-$ 236
126

5

59
23 $+$ 65
29

6

109
63 $-$ 21
67

7

33
11 $\times$ 9
3

8

99
30 $\div$ 10
33

9

6
36 $\times$ 5
30

10

112
63 $\div$ 9
16

11

92
166 $+$ 122
196

12

212
86 $\div$ 43
106

13

23
33 $\times$ 46
66

14

143
99 $-$ 43
87

15

168
84 $\div$ 21
42

16

76
88 $-$ 46
34

17

36
63 $\div$ 21
12

18

81
78 $+$ 42
39

19

96
136 $\div$ 17
12

20

53
75 $+$ 41
63

Exercise 11

1 C	**2** C	**3** B	**4** D	**5** A
6 C	**7** A	**8** D	**9** C	**10** B
11 C	**12** A	**13** B	**14** D	**15** B
16 B	**17** C	**18** C	**19** D	**20** C

Exercise 12

| **1** C | **2** B | **3** C | **4** D | **5** B |
| **6** C | **7** D | **8** A | **9** D | **10** C |

Exercise 13
1    $99 \div 3 + 11 - 18 = 26$
2    $25 \times 4 \div 20 \times 9 = 45$
3    $24 \times 3 + 3 \div = 25$
4    $40 + 8 \times 3 \div 6 = 24$
5    $13 \times 3 + 11 \times 3 = 150$
6    $15 \times 6 + 10 \div 25 = 4$
7    $9 + 5 \times 20 \div 4 = 70$
8    $15 \div 5 \times 8 \div 4 = 6$
9    $19 + 3 \div 2 \div 30 = 3$
10   $19 + 3 \div 2 \times 9 = 99$

2. Flow diagrams (page 161)

Exercise 1

1

2

3

Exercise 2

1   court action
2   reminder sent
3   60 days

Timed flow diagram exercise

1   letter of rejection sent
2   no further action
3   offer of post
4   applicant is invited to sit test
5   details of applicant are passed to management

3. Checking (page 165)

Exercise 1
Those company names with errors have been placed in brackets.

Original	*Copy*
Paine Chocolates	(Pain Chocolates)
Pall Mall Dispensing	Pall Mall Dispensing
Lodge Insurance Brokers	(Lodge Insurence Brokers)
Lodder Est Agts	(LOdder Est Agts)
Mill Hill Dry Clnrs	Mill Hill Dry Clnrs
Kahn Printers	Kahn Printers
Italian Piano Co	Italian Piano Co
Hoxtex Restaurants	(Hoxtex Restaurant)
Apollo Bed and Breakfast	(Apollo Bedand Breakfast)
Holloway Carpenters	Holloway Carpenters
Archway Halal Meat	(Archway Hala Meat)
Hookway Jewellers	Hookway Jewellers
Hi-tec School of Motoring	Hi-tec School of Motoring
Totland Hire Centre	(Totland Hire Center)
George's Recruitment	(Georges Recruitment)
West End Consultants	West End Consultants
Court Cars	(Court cars)
House of Lighting	(Hourse of Lighting)
Woxton Water Works	Woxton Water Works

Castletown Restaurants   (Castletown Recruitments)
Hardwood Doors Group Ltd   (Hardwood Doors Group LTD)
Mike's Do It Yourself Centre   Mike's Do It Yourself Centre
MITAKA Publishing House   (MITAKA Publsihing House)
Sunchung Takeaway   (Sanchung Takeaway)
Move Motorcycle Hire   (Move Motorcyycle Hire)
Portman Car and Van Rental   (Portman Carr and Van Rental)
Heitman and Son Accountants   (Heitman and son Accountance)
Ace Consulting Engineers   Ace Consulting Engineers
Hot Tandoori House   (Hot Tundoori House)
Safe Security Ltd   (Safe security Ltd)

Exercise 2
Original   *Copy*
ABC123   ABC123
ACCB/123/321   ACCB/123/321
CENTIMETRES/CUBIC   (CENTEMETRES/CUBIC)
GUMPTION   GUMPTION
MEASURES/CAPACITY   (MAESURES/CAPACITY)
987654321/123456789   987654321/123456789
987/123/654/456:   (987/123/654/456)
GERMANIUM-72.59   (GERMANUM-72.59)
MOLYBDENUM-95.94   MOLYBDENUM-95.94
NICKEL-58.71   (NICKLE-58.71)
ZIRCONIUM-91.22   ZIRCONIUM-91.22
PHOSPHORUS-30.9738   (PHOSPHOROS-30.9738)
MILLILITRES-36966   (MILLILITERS-36966)
MANGANESE-54.9380   MANGANESE-54.9380
DECAGRAMMES-15432   (DECAGRAMMS-15432)
KILOGRAMME-2205   (KILOGRAMMES-2205)
ANTIMONY-121.75   ANTIMONY-121.75
HYDROGEN-1.0080(H)   (HYDROGIN-1.0080(H))
CHROMIUM-51.996   (CHROMUIM-51.996)
MINNESOTA STATE   (MINNISOTA STATE)
ZEDEKIAH   ZEDEKIAH
WYOMING/CHEYENNE   (WYCOMING/CHEYENNE)
TENNESSEE/NASHVILLE   (TENESSEE/NASHVILLE)

ZOROASTER	ZOROASTER
PENNSYLVANIA/H'BURG	(PENNCYLVANIA/H'BURG)
WHISTLER	(WHISLER)
VERSAILLES	(VERSAILES)
VERRUCOSE	VERRUCOSE
UNHALLOWED	(UNIHALLOWED)
TREACHEROUS	TREACHEROUS
TREASURY	(TREASUERY)
SPARE-PART	(SPAIRE-PART)
ROUSSEAU	(RUOSSEAU)
EQUIVALENTS	(EQIUVALENTS)
FLOUNCE	(FLUONCE)
HARDENBERG	HARDENBERG

Exercise 3

Original	*Copy*
123/456/789/AC	123/456/789/AC
987/654/321/CA	987/654/321/CA
32323/452/CIC	(32332/452/CI(C))
ACEG/818/658	ACEG/818/658
BDFH/4653/12	(BDFH/4653/12)
ZED/678/TLT/010	ZED/678/TLT/010
WORLD/VIEW/83	(WORLD/VEIW/83)
ZEBEDEE/F/JJ	(ZEBFDEE/F/JJ)
YETI/SNOW/MAN	YETI/SNOW/MAN
ORI/GIN/AL/212	ORI/GIN/AL/212
ADVERTISEMENT	(ADVERITISEMENT)
PERSONNEL/DEPT	(PERSENNEL/DEPT)
COM/PUT/ER/SYS/TEM	(COM/PUT/ER/SyS/TEM)
00/11/22/345/678	00/11/22/345/678
3456/0987/4321/32	3456/0987/4321/32
RO/AD/RU/NN/ER/234	(RO/AD/RV/NN/ER/234)
GAL/2001/200001/00	(GAL/2001/20001/00)
ISBN 0–561–15163–0	ISBN 0–561–15163–0
1010101/02020/300	1010101/02020/300
DATA-100/303/404/50	(DATA/100/303/404/50)

4. Coded instructions (2) (page 168)

1	C	**5**	E
2	B	**6**	B
3	D	**7**	D
4	E	**8**	E

5. Coded instructions (3) (page 171)

1	C	**6**	B
2	A	**7**	B
3	B	**8**	D
4	C	**9**	B
5	E	**10**	A

6. Sequencing (page 174)

A	2, 6, 7, 3, 1, 5, 4
B	2, 3, 1, 4
C	4, 2, 1, 3
D	5, 3, 4, 2, 6, 1
E	2, 4, 3, 1
F	3, 2, 1
G	4, 2, 3, 1
H	C
I	Nephew and Aunt
J	S

The sharpest minds need the finest advice. **Kogan Page** creates success.

www.koganpage.com